2/18/92

D0024852

Siting Hazardous Waste Treatment Facilities

Siting Hazardous Waste Treatment Facilities

THE NIMBY SYNDROME

Kent E. Portney

Auburn House
NEW YORK • WESTPORT, CONNECTICUT • LONDON

To Teddy

Library of Congress Cataloging-in-Publication Data

Portney, Kent E.
    Siting hazardous waste treatment facilities : the Nimby Syndrome /
Kent E. Portney.
      p.   cm.
    Includes bibliographical references and index.
    ISBN 0-86569-016-2 (alk. paper)
    1. Hazardous waste treatment facilities—United States—Location—
Public opinion. 2. Hazardous waste treatment facilities—United
States—Location—Citizen participation.   I. Title.
TD1040.P67   1991
363.72'87—dc20   90-1217

British Library Cataloguing in Publication Data is available.

Library of Congress Catalog Card Number: 90-1217
ISBN: 0-86569-016-2

First published in 1991

Auburn House, 88 Post Road West, Westport, CT 06881
An imprint of Greenwood Publishing Group, Inc.

Printed in the United States of America

∞

The paper used in this book complies with the
Permanent Paper Standard issued by the National
Information Standards Organization (Z39.48-1984).

10 9 8 7 6 5 4 3 2 1

Contents

Tables and Figures

TABLES

FIGURES

Preface

This book is about the Not-in-my-backyard (NIMBY) Syndrome and how it affects siting hazardous waste treatment facilities. It investigates the social values and attitudes that underlie the NIMBY Syndrome. In the process, the predominant practices and underlying theories of facility siting are examined, and it is suggested that the processes of siting facilities must be more explicitly thought of as political. What makes this book different from others on siting is that it derives a promising strategy that might facilitate future siting efforts. Indeed, the ultimate objective of this book is to present a type of strategy heretofore not pursued. This strategy, which we call "risk substitution," holds the promise that facilities can be sited without requiring people to change their values or their personal assessments (perceptions) concerning how dangerous it is to live near such a facility. The proposed strategy is not theoretically or conceptually perfect. Most strategies are not. But it responds to the idea that if something works in practice, it will probably work in theory.

Perhaps the most difficult aspect of putting forth a potentially effective strategy is the possible "downside" or consequences of that strategy. Indeed, the idea is predicated on the assumption, whether reasonable or not, that hazardous waste treatment facilities can and will be made safer than the currently practiced alternatives—relying on a variety of disposal techniques including landfill. Most people would probably agree that hazardous waste reduction is a preferable course of action. One of the possible downsides to a successful risk substitution strategy might be the undermining of existing incentives for producers of hazardous wastes to seek source reduction. However, as noted in the text, the risk substitution strategy is developed under the assumption that source reduction, by itself, is inadequate to the task of protecting the environment from hazardous wastes. Thus, the motivation behind this book is a desire to improve the quality of our environment.

This book does not advocate siting hazardous waste treatment facilities in any specific place. It does, however, prescribe some ways of identifying places where siting would most likely be successful because it presents a methodology for anticipating local political opposition. Ultimately, the foundational value of this book is that siting facilities in places where people do not want them is, has to be, fundamentally wrong. Unless people, especially the people most directly affected, accept these facilities, then the siting process and result must be considered less than optimum.

Acknowledgments

I would like to thank several people without whose assistance and contributions this book would have been a much more difficult or impossible task. First, I would like to thank the many people who contributed to the survey research reported herein—particularly Ken Thomson of the Lincoln Filene Center for Citizenship and Public Affairs, who assisted in the design and implementation of the survey projects; and the numerous students at Tufts who actually conducted the hundreds of interviews. Additionally, I am also grateful to: Stuart Langton, former Executive Director of the Lincoln Filene Center, for his efforts in securing funding to support this research; Harry Fatkin of the Polaroid Corporation for helping to arrange financial support from the Polaroid Foundation; and Tony Cortese, Dean of Environmental Programs at Tufts, for the support provided through the Tufts Center for Environmental Management.

Two people in particular deserve special thanks for their role in the publication of this book. These include John Harney of Auburn House, who convinced me that his imprint was the appropriate one for this book; and Meg Fergusson of the Greenwood Publishing Group, the production editor whose editorial prowess helped overcome near disaster after United Parcel Service lost the original copyedited manuscript.

Chapter 1

Some Pieces to the Hazardous Waste Treatment Facility Siting Puzzle

In recent years, there has been an inordinate amount of scholarly and applied attention paid to the issue of whether, and where, to site hazardous waste treatment facilities in the United States. The issue of facility siting has been elevated in relative importance on the public agenda because of a variety of simultaneously acting events. Through the decade of the 1970's and into the 1980's, our national environmental awareness fueled concern about the dangers that lurk under our ground and in our water. The more we learned the more frightened we became. To some degree, our fears fed short-term public policy actions which actually made the problem worse. If this weren't bad enough, our fears also prevented our policy makers from pursuing solutions that could actually diminish the dangers.

This makes it sound as though the general society or entire populace is somehow responsible for the hazardous waste mess we face today. It is tempting simply to chalk up this seemingly intractable problem as being one where our public officials are irresponsibly acting as a mirror of the general public. We could cite this as another example of what happens when our governments function as populist democracies. However, this is not an accurate reflection of the full picture in this puzzle. Our fears about proposed public policy solutions to hazardous waste problems may be well founded. Indeed, when one examines the full picture within its political and social context, it is difficult to find fault with the seeming logic that underlies our policy decisions. Given the political and social context in which public hazardous waste-related policy decisions have been made, both at the federal and state levels, these decisions do not appear that unreasonable. Moreover, our current policies, whatever they may be said to be, do represent a sort of failure or shortcoming of contemporary American democracy.

Attempts to address hazardous waste problems have contained some of the most profoundly conflictual events experienced today. Yet our public decision-making processes have not been able to adequately deal with this conflict. Again, it is not that public officials, especially elected officials, simply bow to public pressure in deciding what to do and how to do it. Rather, it is that there is virtually no viable alternative. Because the courses of action already pursued will not prove adequate to solving the hazardous waste problem, we need to develop a deeper understanding of what must change to allow us to pursue effective policies. We have chosen the "puzzle" metaphor to describe the current state of knowledge about siting hazardous waste treatment facilities, about why various approaches seem to have failed, and about what can be done to make treatment facilities a realistic part of a larger policy of managing toxic wastes. Let us look at some of the pieces of the puzzle by first understanding how we arrived at our current position.

ENVIRONMENTAL FEARS AND PUBLIC POLICY RESPONSES

It is not possible to know precisely when we started to develop a deep concern, even a fear, about our physical environment. Obviously, much of it was the result of the numerous environmental catastrophes of the 1960's and 1970's. News reports of the oil spill off the coast of Santa Barbara, the fire on the Cuyahuga River in Cleveland, Ohio, the near-death of some of the Great Lakes, and recognition of the damage produced by pesticides such as DDT through works such as Rachel Carson's

Silent Spring, all gave rise to a general public concern about the quality of our physical environment. Of course, we cannot discount the impact of the nuclear power plant accidents at Three Mile Island in Pennsylvania and Chernobyl in the Soviet Union.

Public attention probably began to focus on the disposal of toxic wastes with the revelations about apparent health effects in Love Canal, New York, where an entire neighborhood slowly manifested common, unexplainable ailments (Levine, 1982). It took years for the people to become mobilized and obtain any sort of positive response and recognition from public officials. As the general public learned of the events surrounding Love Canal, our naivete was replaced by a sense of distrust of how American industries were handling hazardous substances and skepticism about the efficacy of the public sector to regulate them.

This distrust of industry, along with a recognition that government should do more to learn about how serious the hazardous waste problem really was, at least in part bears responsibility for several major pieces of federal legislation beginning in the mid-1970's. The first of these, the Resource Conservation and Recovery Act of 1976 (RCRA), was designed to ensure that hazardous substances were not disposed of without regard for potential public health consequences. It did this, in part, by requiring the tracking of hazardous substances from the time they are created until the time they are disposed, or from their "cradle to grave." This act was altered in 1984 with the Hazardous and Solid Waste Amendments, which clarified and extended the Environmental Protection Agency's (EPA) jurisdiction over the regulation of hazardous wastes.

Another major piece of legislation, the Comprehensive Environmental Response, Compensation, and Liability Act of 1980 (CERCLA), established what has become known as the "superfund" to help finance clean-up of hazardous waste sites and chemical spills. It also established liability in the law for recovery of clean-up costs from responsible parties. This law also required the federal implementing agency, the Environmental Protection Agency, to establish a priority listing of hazardous waste sites that needed to be cleaned up. These were our first real national public policy responses to the elevated place that hazardous waste issues assumed on the public agenda.

Subsequently, Congress passed the Superfund Amendments and Reauthorization Act of 1986, which as the name implies, reauthorized EPA to identify and take actions on hazardous waste sites. The Act also required that EPA set clear standards in their regulations as to who is responsible for site clean-up, how clean the site has to be, and how to select the technological method to clean up the site. Part of what motivated Congress' call for such clear standards was the growing recognition that in implementing site clean-ups, many problems were actually made worse. Additionally, the growing body of case law on the liability established by the Superfund Acts suggests that it is becoming increasingly difficult for corporate officials and employees to avoid responsibility for illegal disposal of hazardous substances. The law allows individuals and corporations to be held criminally liable even if they themselves did not commit the act of illegal disposal.

As the EPA began to focus much of its effort on fulfilling the spirit of the CERCLA and its successor legislation through implementing the superfund for hazardous waste cleanups, we became increasingly knowledgeable and alarmed about the magnitude of the existing hazardous waste problem in the United States. Here was an agency of the federal government identifying physical locations around the country that posed perhaps immediate dangers to our health. A perusal of the Superfund priority list shows that there is scarcely an area of the country that is not affected by the hazardous waste problem. When an area, or "site," appears on the priority list you can be sure that it is not lost on the local media. The message to people is clear: there is a new danger to their health.

In addition to the growing perception of threats from the irresponsible handling of hazardous chemicals, numerous other threats to our environment compound the problem in many people's minds. In 1978, there was a major nuclear power plant accident at Three Mile Island, near Harrisburg, Pennsylvania.

Clearly, people's perceptions about nuclear power changed drastically and perhaps permanently (Freudenberg and Baxter, 1984). Then the massive nuclear power plant catastrophe at Chernobyl in the Soviet Union acted to reinforce our sense of a serious environmental threat. At the same time, public discussion began to address the question of what to do with all the high-level nuclear waste produced by those nuclear power plants. You might wonder what this has to do with hazardous chemical wastes. For whatever reasons, most people do not automatically discriminate among different forms of hazardous wastes. People's perceptions about threats to environmental health from hazardous substances of all types tend to be merged together. Thus, perceptions about nuclear power's dangers affect and are affected by perceptions about the dangers of hazardous chemical wastes.

There is no question but that all of these events have combined to increase our awareness of environmental dangers. Perhaps ironically, this increased awareness has both increased the pressure on our political system to diminish the dangers and decreased the options that our policy makers can pursue. In a sense, our increased awareness has made solving the "hazardous waste problem" a public policy imperative while making it impossible to do so in practice. We will see how and why this has occurred.

THE SEARCH FOR PUBLIC SOLUTIONS

All of these events helped to move hazardous waste problems squarely onto the public agenda. To a degree never experienced before, public officials and industry began to search for some solution to this problem. Of course not everyone perceived that there was in fact a problem. But by and large, by the early 1980's there had developed a fairly clear consensus that steps would have to be taken to alleviate the health threat from toxic chemicals.

This is not to say that everyone agreed on which chemicals are toxic or at what levels. Not everyone agreed about the pace with which action should be taken. Moreover, as an extension of the Reagan administration's simultaneous pursuit of overall deregulation and shift of responsibilities from the federal to state governments, people disagreed about the role of the federal EPA in toxics policy (Cohen, 1984). Nevertheless, some degree of consensus developed that something had to be done.

This consensus seemed to focus on at least four major types of solutions. Initially, the immediate concern focused on cleaning up existing toxic threats. Thus, Superfund was born, with the notion that hazardous waste sites would be identified, analyzed, and cleaned up. However, it was also recognized that this approach did nothing for addressing the problem of future threats. Clearly, the existing threats were seen as the product of the poor practices of the past, and unless these practices were changed in the present, the problems would continue into the future.

Thus, additional attention turned on what is usually called "waste minimization" or "source reduction" technologies. This second solution simply reflects the idea that too much hazardous chemical waste is being produced and that the magnitude of the problem can be reduced perhaps to a more manageable level by diminishing the amounts of chemical wastes requiring disposal. Much of this focuses on incentives for getting industry to alter its manufacturing processes so that less toxic waste is produced as byproducts. Simultaneously, it calls for sanctions (as manifested in clearly fixed liability found, for example, in the CERCLA) for producers of hazardous chemical wastes to dispose of wastes properly. It also focuses on getting people to understand that a large portion of the problem of improper chemical waste disposal comes from the home. Many people seemed to believe that source reduction might by itself constitute a complete solution to the problems of the future. Yet at some point numerous studies made it fairly clear that by merely altering the various manufacturing and technical processes and practices that produced hazardous chemical wastes within the home, we would not likely reduce the stream of hazardous wastes to a manageable level given existing technologies (O'Hare, 1984).

The third type of solution called for increasing corporate accountability in the handling of hazardous chemical wastes. This approach was stimulated by the belief that producers of hazardous chemical wastes were essentially acting irresponsibly by burying their problems underground or dumping them into our waterways. Thus, the obvious answer was to regulate the handling of such wastes by requiring producers to account for what they did with them as was required under the RCRA. Additionally, major efforts were made to license landfills so that only those which could reasonably be said to be "secure," or unlikely to allow toxic chemicals buried there to leach into the groundwater or otherwise become health dangers, would be allowed to accept them. Increasingly, enforcement of landfill disposal regulations closed off disposal options for producers. This, naturally, stimulated attempts to find alternative disposal methodologies.

This leads us to the fourth solution, developing hazardous waste treatment facilities. Under this solution, chemical wastes would be subjected to chemical processes which would render them non-toxic, or at least less toxic than before. In most cases, the products of such processes could be safely disposed of in the final instance through such existing techniques as landfills. The chemical processes to which toxic substances would be subjected, of course, would vary widely depending on the toxic in question. In some cases, re-usable industrial products would be extracted and re-sold, as with solvent recovery plants. In other cases, toxics would be incinerated at very high temperatures to render them less toxic. Different processes would be applied to different toxic chemicals.

Most of the states have bought into the idea that licensing the construction and operation of hazardous waste treatment facilities holds great promise for solving (or avoiding) the future problem, although the states vary a great deal in the amount of effort they put into this approach (Bowman, 1984, 1985). However, in practice few if any of such facilities have been built. We do not yet have a full understanding of why we have been so incapable of implementing this type of solution. There are many plausible explanations. We usually attribute such failures to the pervasive Not-in-my-backyard, or NIMBY, Syndrome. Other explanations attribute this failure to the lack of public participation in siting processes and, perhaps paradoxically, to having too much public participation. Sometimes the inability to site facilities is blamed on the lack of public leadership in helping to resolve local siting conflicts. Still other explanations point to the widespread decline in trust in both our public and private sector institutions. But none of these explanations is accompanied by clear or credible prescriptions for remedying the siting problem. For example, even if decline in public trust were directly responsible for the failure to site facilities, what could be done to overcome this? It does not seem particularly realistic to await the re-building of that trust in government before trying to site treatment facilities. So we need to develop some clearer explanations of why public opposition persists, or at least explanations that are somewhat more empirically tied to possible prescriptions.

SITING AS A STATE POLICY PROBLEM

The states have pursued a number of different approaches to siting treatment facilities (Hadden, Veillette, and Brandt, 1983; Ryan, 1984; Wells, 1982; O'Hare, Bacow, and Sanderson, 1983; USEPA, 1979). These methods are not greatly different from those pursued in regulating the siting of many other types of environmentally impacting industrial plants (Duerksen, 1983). Each method attempts to anticipate the public opposition implied by the NIMBY syndrome. The methods employed by the various states may attempt to suppress, ignore, or respond to such opposition. Perhaps due to the unworkability of most of these approaches, states have often changed the laws governing treatment facility siting. Consequently, it is somewhat difficult to provide an accurate and timely picture of where the states stand at any given time. However, we can provide a brief summary of the types of approaches that have been attempted in the states at some time over the last decade or so.

The Pre-Emptive Approach

One method, pursued by twelve states at one time or another, including Illinois, Maryland, and Florida, is to consolidate the siting authority in a state agency or a state siting board with no community representation. This method, which can actually take several different forms, recognizes that facility siting will likely be opposed by any community in which it is proposed. This state agency has the authority, in theory, to overrule the local opposition in the interest of the general population of the state. This is often referred to as "pre-emption" of local authority. In theory, while local citizens and officials may have some input into the process, they have no veto power over the ultimate decision, which rests in the state agency.

Although it is conceivable that this pre-emption could occur, in fact it, by and large, has not. For example, a study by Morell and Magorian (1982) of the siting process shows that the bureaucratic dynamics and governing values operated to ensure that local opinion was not overruled by the state agency. Additionally, local residents are often able to generate political influence to prevent siting (Andrews and Pierson, 1985; 1984). Thus, this type of statute has proven to be no more effective than any other statute in providing a way of siting treatment facilities.

The State Authority with Local Input Approach

Some states rely on an approach to siting which provides some input from the community in which a facility is proposed to be built. In this approach, local citizens or local officials are often given positions on a statewide siting board or on a statewide waste management planning council. States such as Florida and New Jersey rely on this approach.

Ostensibly, local interests are taken into consideration through participation in the process. The implication is that the local input is only one of many different points of view or interests which ultimately determine siting decisions.

The Local Involvement and Influence Approach

Another technique for siting facilities provides local officials and citizens with substantial influence over the siting process. One form of this approach provides an opportunity for local citizens and officials to negotiate with the developer proposing to build a treatment facility. Another form provides local communities with a veto or near-veto power over siting decisions.

This approach, used by at least four states (Connecticut, Rhode Island, Massachusetts, and Wisconsin), is based on two separate sets of value-based assumptions. The first assumption is that local decision making should not be pre-empted. This recognizes the sanctity, found in the traditions of many states, of local politics and government. The second assumption is that people oppose the siting of treatment facilities for very rational reasons. This assumption is based on the notion that the people in a community where a treatment facility is proposed to be built experience a very different set of personal benefits and burdens than people elsewhere.

Unlike most approaches to facility siting, the form of this approach, which provides for negotiation and mediation, is based soundly on prescriptions about the most effective way to allay public opposition. These prescriptions are derived from a type of economic theory often referred to as the economic theory of compensation (O'Hare, 1977). The siting laws based on this approach prescribe that in theory the remedy to opposition can be found in the theory of economic compensation (O'Hare, Bacow, and Sanderson, 1983). We will discuss this approach more fully in Chapter 2.

FACILITY SITING AND THE NIMBY SYNDROME

Public opposition to facility siting has now reached the point where it has been given status as a full-scale public malady—the NIMBY, or Not-in-my-backyard, Syndrome. The NIMBY Syndrome is a phenomenon based on a conceptual attempt to capture the idea that this kind of public opposition is different from more general opposition (Armour, 1984; Edelstein, 1988: 170–189). The NIMBY Syndrome is a reflection of a public attitude that seems to be almost self-contradictory—that people feel it is desirable to site a particular type of facility somewhere as long as it is not where they personally live. The NIMBY Syndrome concept usually does not apply to attitudes of general opposition.

Contemporary siting of public prisons is perhaps an apt example of the NIMBY Syndrome. Nearly everyone seems to agree that more prison space is needed if the criminal justice system is to be able to treat convicted criminals as harshly as the public mood warrants. Yet no one wants a prison in his or her city or town. Siting hazardous waste treatment facilities is a specific type of facility siting that is not all that different from that of prisons. Most people seem to agree that such facilities are a necessary and acceptable result of living in an industrial society.

We can illustrate this type of pattern of attitudes with the assistance of survey research results. Figure 1.1 and Table 1.1 show the results from public opinion surveys in Massachusetts and the nation, which we will describe more fully later in this chapter. This Figure and Table show that a majority of the people in the samples clearly feel that hazardous waste treatment facilities should be sited somewhere. In combined Massachusetts surveys from five cities and towns, over fifty-six percent of the respondents said that they favored building a treatment facility somewhere in the state. In a nationwide survey, a little over fifty percent of the people said they favored siting a facility somewhere in their respective states. Yet when the issue becomes one of siting the facility in people's respective cities or towns, the NIMBY Syndrome rears its ugly head, as reflected in the fact that attitudes do an about-face. In the combined Massachusetts surveys, less than a third of the people favored siting a treatment facility in their respective cities or towns. In the nationwide survey, less than eighteen percent of the people favored placing the facility in their communities.

Figure 1.1
Attitudes Toward Siting: Opposition to Statewide Versus Local Facility Siting

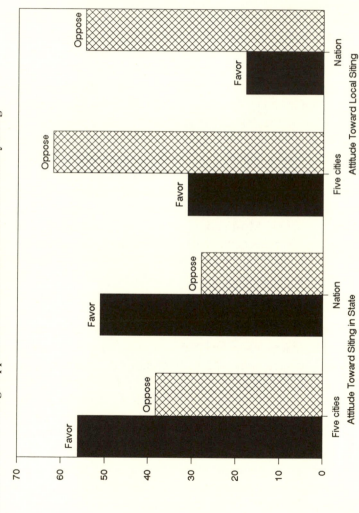

Table 1.1
Public Attitudes Toward Siting Hazardous Waste Treatment Facilities

	Favor or Mostly favor	Oppose or Mostly oppose	Don't know	Total
Attitude toward building treatment facility in Massachusetts, five city sample [a]	56.1%	38.3%	6.6%	100.0%
Attitude toward building treatment facility in respondent's state, national sample [b]	51.1%	28.0%	20.9%	100.0%
Attitude toward building treatment facility in respondent's city or town, Massachusetts sample [c]	31.1%	61.9%	7.0%	100.0%
Attitude toward building treatment facility in respondent's city or town, national sample [d]	17.8%	54.6%	27.6%	100.0%

[a] The results shown here are an aggregation of the five city-based surveys in Massachusetts. These city-based surveys are described in the text. Question wording: A number of companies have expressed the desire to build a hazardous waste treatment plant in Massachusetts. A hazardous waste treatment plant is a factory which tries to change hazardous waste into safe waste. A hazardous waste treatment plant does not bury wastes in any way. Would you say you favor having a company build a plant in Massachusetts, neither favor or oppose it, oppose it, or what? For those answering "neither" or "don't know," we asked: Would you say you mostly favor or mostly oppose such a plant?

[b] Results are from the nationwide survey. The question wording is essentially the same as that used for the Massachusetts surveys except that "your state" was substituted for "Massachusetts."

[c] The results shown here are an aggregation of the five city-based surveys in Massachusetts. The question asked was a follow-up to the question described above, and was worded as: What about in [respondent's city or town name]? Would you say you favor having a company build a hazardous waste treatment plant in [respondent's city or town], neither favor nor oppose it, oppose it, or what? Again, for those answering "neither" or "don't know," we asked: Would you say you mostly favor or mostly oppose such a plant?

[d] The question wording is the same as that used in the Massachusetts surveys.

One might argue that these attitudes do not really matter very much, especially if people keep their attitudes to themselves. Yet there is increasing evidence that the NIMBY Syndrome has given rise to a variety of new types of political behavior, often serving as a catalyst mobilizing people to be politically active. For example, attempts to site locally unwanted land uses, or LULUs, have produced no end of local citizen groups focused on blocking those land uses (Bachrach and Zautra, 1985; Edelstein, 1988: 84–87). One only needs to cite the examples of court-ordered low income housing in Yonkers, New York, or the attempt to locate a new prison facility in New Braintree, Massachusetts, as examples. In many cases, such mobilized opposition has lead to rather boisterous public confrontations, such as the public hearing that degenerates into a shouting match or even a brawl. Becoming politically active in response to something perceived of as a community threat appears to constitute a common form of "coping mechanism" for the people who face that threat (Edelstein, 1988: 84–87).

To many, the mobilization of public opposition is nothing more than democracy in action. It is the result of citizens exercising their constitutional right to participate in their governmental decisions. To others, this mobilization reflects public participation at its worst, democracy rearing its ugly head. To these latter people, it is the result of an over-extension of democracy essentially giving citizens the authority to make decisions in areas they don't understand. Thus, the NIMBY Syndrome carries with it serious implications about how facilities are and should be sited in a democracy (MacDonald, 1984).

HAZARDOUS WASTE POLICY AS A PROBLEM FOR DEMOCRACY

Perhaps the most compelling explanation for our inability to deal with the hazardous waste problem in the United States is that our system of democracy has not been able to meet the challenge. We, of course, like to believe that our particular form of democratic decision making is beyond reproach. Yet when the puzzle approaches being fully assembled, we begin to see a picture in which some of the elements that characterize our contemporary democracy and in some sense give it its strength, can also be said to limit our ability to effectively address environmental hazards. For example, because we have never felt comfortable specifying precisely at which level of government specific types of problems should be resolved, we find that there is direct conflict between local democratic decisions and democratic decisions made at the state, regional, or federal level. In this case, deference to local forms of democracy ensures that decisions made democratically at the state or federal level will never be carried out.

But it is not enough to argue that our current policies and practices are the result of tension among competing interests in the larger American polity. Similarly, it is not particularly valuable to indict our form of democratic decision making. There certainly would be nothing very profound or new about this. Indeed, the problem we have described has become more generally known as "policy stalemate" or policy "gridlock" and has been observed in many other public policy or program areas. The more important point is that because our system is not particularly capable of producing resolution of issues like the hazardous waste problem, we are perhaps inadvertently drawn toward the conclusion that some problems cannot be resolved democratically, that is, through a participatory process that is considered by us as Americans to be fair and legitimate.

The underlying argument in this book is that once we understand what motivates the full array of attitudes toward hazardous waste policy, especially treatment facility siting, *and* the political constraints placed on the search for solutions, reasonable solutions are still available. Solutions calling for abandoning all methods that generate hazardous waste are perhaps premature, and prescriptions which blatantly circumvent one or another element of our admittedly fragmented democratic society cannot hope to provide durable answers. Instead, answers must take into consideration very real conflicts among people who have extremely intense attitudes and beliefs about the problem.

Before this argument can be said to be credible, we need to look at some of the many explanations that have been offered for why resolution of the hazardous waste problem has been so difficult and reflect on some new ones. The effort here is devoted to the idea that many of these explanations constitute pieces in a sort of puzzle. Once we understand how these pieces fit together, we can begin to prescribe what it would take to make the hazardous waste treatment facility a practicing, albeit partial, solution to the problem of toxic chemical wastes. Additionally, we will argue that many of this puzzle's pieces have been misread and consequently have led to policy and program prescriptions which are doomed to fail.

THE LAYOUT OF THE ARGUMENTS

What follows herein is a series of arguments which help to construct a picture of the sources of and possible answers to the seemingly intractable problem of hazardous waste treatment facility siting. The overall argument is that once we understand some of the errors of past policy and practice, we can begin to be more sensitive to those policy alternatives which have a chance of working. In Chapter 2 we focus on several very common attempts to intervene in public opposition to facility siting, with special emphasis on the errors of logic and inference that led us in the past to believe that some factors were causal when *ex post facto* they seem clearly not to be.

At least partly because we have been mistaken about the causes of public opposition, we have proceeded to pursue what I refer to as "political approaches" to facility siting that themselves are flawed. By this I mean that they prescribe siting processes which are based on unreasonable or unwarranted assumptions about who should and who should not participate in the process in order to make siting happen. Chapter 3 investigates some of these political processes and why the assumptions have been flawed. Perhaps more importantly, this chapter argues that when one merges what we know about public opposition with what we know about political processes, many of the currently proposed policies and approaches are just as likely to fail as their predecessors. None of the proposals seems very likely to produce changes in people's attitudes toward siting. In particular, neither excluding major political interests, nor including them in some form of citizen participation process, are likely to reduce the level of public opposition.

This still leaves unanswered the question of what can be done, if anything, to change people's attitudes toward local siting. Addressing this question requires empirical analysis of the correlates of changes in people's attitudes. Chapters 4 and 5 present some basic analysis of this type as an empirical first step in sorting out the possible causes of public opposition and attitudinal change.

Once we begin to understand the underlying correlates and causes of public attitudes and changes in these attitudes (or the lack thereof), we can begin to develop a clearer idea of what kinds of policies and programs are likely to produce successful facility siting. Chapter 6 places the problem of facility siting into a broader psychological, political, and social context. Relying on notions of the social construction of risk, this chapter argues that the patterns of opposition to facility siting are reflective of a broader pattern of political, social, and psychological attitudes about the environment. It is this context which helps to define what is acceptable or unacceptable when it comes to the risks of living near a hazardous waste treatment facility. The conclusion drawn from these chapters is that it may well be unreasonable to expect people to change their perceptions of risk. In other words, if siting methodologies require people to change their attitudes, perceptions, or values, siting is extremely unlikely to occur.

Finally, Chapter 7 outlines one major proposal or framework, the result of a special effort to link causal inferences with the proposal. The ultimate argument found in this chapter is that political and policy reform must take into consideration what we know about the public's perceptions of the relative risks of facility siting within their broader political and social contexts. Relying on what we already know about people's preferences for risk aversion, we begin to develop a central proposal seemingly capable of producing successful siting. This chapter develops the idea of "risk substitution" as a proposal for addressing locally unwanted facilities, especially waste treatment facilities, and suggests that this may be the only systematic way of confronting local opposition.

It is hoped that one broad message will come through from this work. Responding to the need for hazardous waste treatment facilities cannot be accomplished in a local political vacuum. It makes no sense to ignore the political realities produced by local opposition. It also makes little sense to ignore the underlying perceptual roots of that local opposition. Solutions to the problems of siting noxious facilities must account for and incorporate rather than circumvent the political realities that will inevitably be faced.

THE DATA USED IN THE ARGUMENTS

Most of the arguments found in the following chapters are supported by analysis of original data. These data are the result of several years of study conducted by the Citizen Survey Program at the Lincoln Filene Center for Citizenship and Public Affairs, Tufts University. The data were derived from two different major public opinion surveys during 1983 and 1984.

The first of these surveys, funded by a grant from the Polaroid Foundation, focused on attitudes and perceptions of the general public in five Massachusetts cities and towns. In each of these cities and towns, Brockton, Chelsea, Newton, Sturbridge, and Ware, a sample of a little over three hundred residents was selected and extensive telephone interviews were conducted. The cities and towns in this study were selected from among a list of all cities and towns in the state. After establishing selection criteria designed to maximize selection of communities most likely to provide unbiased data, the communities were examined and the list was narrowed down. For example, one criterion precluded selection of any community which had experienced any sort of major environmental crisis, such as a toxic chemical spill, discovery of an EPA Superfund priority landfill, and so on.

The second major project, funded by a grant from Tufts University's Center for Environmental Management, involved a similar survey relying on a sample of some 564 U.S. citizens from the 48 contiguous states and the District of Columbia. This survey was designed to provide some specific baseline information against which the Massachusetts survey results could be compared. Moreover, it was intended to provide some insight into people's perceptions and attitudes nationally.

Why Focus on Citizens?

The focus on citizens as the units of analysis is governed by the fact that individuals' attitudinal opposition to hazardous waste treatment facility siting and perceptions of risk are the important concepts in this study. Many other studies have focused on local community or political activists' attitudes or perceptions. While these perceptions are undoubtedly important in understanding the political reactions to facility siting efforts, we wanted to investigate possible antecedents to such activism. In particular, we wanted to focus on the nature of general population (such as community) perceptions of risk with the idea that perhaps eventually we could link these perceptions to the emergence of community activists. In order to accomplish the task of characterizing whole populations, a representative sample of citizens is required.

Why Rely on Six Different Samples?

The six different samples provide us with an opportunity to investigate several important aspects of citizens' attitudes toward hazardous waste treatment facility siting and related issues. Five of the samples are based on local governmental jurisdictions. The sixth sample is nationwide.

The five local samples of cities and towns permit us to examine hazardous waste treatment facility siting as a local issue. The principal focus of this research was on the NIMBY syndrome. This implies a local orientation, although the exact definition of what is local (for example, what constitutes "my backyard") is not clear. It is clear, however, that this kind of issue is very much a local issue.

The cities and towns included in the surveys were selected because they represent a range of aggregate characteristics. For example, we selected cities with fairly low, moderate, and high median family incomes. Thus, having an array of cities and towns permits us to examine the differences among different kinds of towns. In particular, the city and town samples allowed us to examine whether the NIMBY Syndrome manifests itself differently in different kinds of local areas.

Just as there are advantages associated with relying on local samples, so too are there disadvantages. We would like to develop some information about how generalizable whatever patterns we find are. For example, if we find that in the local samples that people of higher incomes are less likely to accept the siting of a hazardous waste treatment facility, this tells us only about this sample. We cannot say with any confidence that higher income people in our local samples are in any way representative of higher income people elsewhere. The results from the local samples do not necessarily tell us anything about how people from other areas feel. The nationwide sample provides us with an opportunity to assess how generalizable the patterns are.

We will use the local and nationwide samples in another way. In some instances, the local samples' results will raise questions which ought to be addressed. The national sample will be used to bring some data to bear on some of these questions. For example, the local samples might raise a question about misperceptions of the risks associated with living near a hazardous waste treatment facility compared to the risks of living near some other relatively hazardous facility. Because the surveys of people in these local samples did not ask respondents to provide information about such risks, these samples cannot be used to evaluate such a question. However, the nationwide sample does provide us with responses to questions about perceptions of the relative risks associated with living near a variety of dangerous facilities. Thus, the nationwide sample will be used to augment information developed in the analysis of the local samples.

Disadvantages of the Survey Technique

Just as we hope that relying on the results of survey research will yield some important insights, it is clear that this technique may not be an effective way of getting at some questions. As we will discuss in subsequent chapters, some of the questions we asked of respondents required answers to hypothetical situations. This is not a problem with using survey research per se, but may be a shortcoming in its present application. It is, of course, impossible to know whether these answers provide an accurate reflection of what would transpire in actual situations. For example, we asked people to tell us how they think they would react if a proposal were put forth to build a treatment plant in their neighborhood. Respondents did not hesitate to tell us how they thought they would react. But whether this is how they would actually react is impossible to know with the available data.

An additional disadvantage must be addressed. In some of our analysis we rely on responses to questions about preferences. For example, we asked people to tell us whether they would prefer to live near a hazardous waste treatment plant or an airport. While we made every effort to ensure that the answers people provided are accurate, it is possible that respondents intentionally disguise their true preferences. Preference revelation is difficult to achieve in survey research. However, the surveys were conducted in a way that attempted to minimize the extent to which this is a problem. We will address the specifics of these problems at various points in the analysis.

IMPLICATIONS FOR OTHER TYPES OF
FACILITY SITING

While the primary intent here is to provide information specifically relevant to hazardous waste treatment facility siting, the results may well have implications for other types of environmentally impacting facility siting attempts. The siting of hazardous waste treatment facilities undoubtedly possesses some unique characteristics, but there is also much to learn from past successful experiences with the siting of other types of facilities. Similarly, as we learn more about hazardous waste treatment facility siting, we may be able to formulate prescriptions about other types of facilities.

It is not uncommon today for serious social and political conflicts to arise out of seemingly mundane attempts to site such facilities as city or town landfills, power plants (whether nuclear powered or not), trash-to-energy plants, prisons, industrial parks, and so on. In many instances, local residents become pitted against other residents, against businesses, and against government agencies in a desire to block the siting of such facilities. Although we would not wish to argue that any one of these facilities by itself is critical, ultimately the inability to site such facilities raises questions about the effects on limiting economic growth and development. The results of this research may begin to help us understand many of these other types of locally based action potentially threatened by citizen opposition.

With this in mind we can turn our attention to how the public dilemma, characterized by the need for environmentally noxious facilities and local opposition which precludes such facilities, manifests itself.

Chapter 2

Understanding the Hazardous Waste Dilemma: What Works and What Doesn't Work in Hazardous Waste Treatment Facility Siting

We undoubtedly have a clear understanding of the fact that our public institutions today simultaneously feel pressured to react responsibly on the issue of hazardous chemical wastes and feel stymied in their attempts to do so. Practically every state in the country has accepted the fact that relying on hazardous waste treatment facilities is a major part of any responsible public attempt to reduce environmental risks from the disposal of dangerous chemicals. Yet all of these states have experienced the impossibility or at least a high degree of difficulty in siting such facilities. This is the hazardous waste dilemma in a nutshell.

Unfortunately, this description of the dilemma does not take us very far in developing an understanding of how we have arrived at the point where such a dilemma seems to exist. To begin to develop this understanding, we must start by examining what works and what does not work in successful hazardous waste treatment facility siting. Such an examination inevitably concentrates on what does not work because, simply stated, nothing yet identified seems to have worked with any degree of consistency. Because of this fact, our attention then shifts to why it is that none of the policy responses has produced the kind of changes in public attitudes needed to site treatment facilities. In the process of conducting this examination, it will become clear that virtually none of the policy alternatives pursued to date has been informed by any reliable understanding of what causes people to oppose the siting of treatment facilities. Nearly all of the proposals rely on assumptions or inferences about the public which are not supportable by existing empirical evidence. Moreover, as we will see in this chapter, as well as in Chapters 3 and 4, it is difficult to escape the conclusion that many of these proposals flow from inaccurate inferences about what causes public opposition in the first place.

Our attention in this chapter focuses on the what might be called the major "apolitical" proposals to permit and encourage success-ful facility siting. By "apolitical" we mean those intervention proposals that attempt to produce changes in attitudes and/or behavior seemingly without reference to facility siting as involv-ing a political process. For the most part, these proposals address public attitudes and behavior in what might appear to be a rather mechanistic way, sometimes stressing the psychological or social context but not the political context of such attitudes and behavior. This chapter also focuses on the assumptions and inferences about peoples' attitudes and perceptions that seem to underlie the major "apolitical" proposals and policies that have been pursued to date.

THEORY VERSUS PRACTICE

Contradictions Between Expectations and Experiences

The relatively short history of attempts to site hazardous waste treatment facilities provides abundant documentation of the frus-tration of effective policy. By now it seems clear that the literature on facility siting is replete with seeming contradictions. Many works develop theoretical or quasi-theoretical prescriptions to inform the siting process. Other works document the pervasive difficulty of implementing these prescriptions in practice. In short, it almost seems that for every proposal about how siting should take place there is empirical evidence that it will not, or does not, work with any degree of consistency in practice. In order to demonstrate this, we can take a brief look at several of the more commonly pursued proposals which would enable treatment facility siting to take place, and we can contrast these proposals with analyses of their effectiveness.

ECONOMIC COMPENSATION AND FINANCIAL INCENTIVES

Promising Theory and Disappointing Results

The economic theory of compensation in siting facilities which are perceived by nearby residents to present risks is largely based on the provision of economic incentives and compensating people for the actual or perceived costs they must bear. It starts with the assumption that public opposition stems from a basic imbalance in people's individual benefit-risk calculations (Hadden and Hazelton, 1980; Mitchell and Carson, 1986). The idea is that opposition to the siting of facilities comes from people in close proximity to the site because these people are being asked to bear the high personal costs (in the form of risk) while the benefits of the facility accrue to a larger outside population.

O'Hare's important theoretical work delineated the role of compensation in redressing this imbalance (1977). His analysis argues that economic incentives could be offered to local residents so that perceived benefits would eventually outweigh the perceived risks. Thus, the imbalance would be redressed, and public opposition would abate. Evolving from this argument are numerous discussions of techniques designed to mitigate or manage social risk assessment. Thus, the focus has become one of attempting to devise methods of altering people's subjective assessments of the benefits relative to risks associated with living near potentially noxious facilities.

The economic theory is fairly straightforward. It suggests that people make personal benefit-cost or benefit-risk calculations about having a treatment facility located near their homes. If the personal benefits outweigh the personal costs or risks, they will approve of the facility. If, as is usually the case, people estimate that the costs or risks are higher than the benefits (that net costs are relatively high), they will oppose the facility (O'Hare, Bacow, and Sanderson, 1983: 73; O'Hare, 1977).

Under this theory, it would be perfectly rational for people to seek the benefits of a facility while avoiding bearing the costs or risks. Thus, we would expect people who see that there are benefits to such a facility to favor building one somewhere. Siting such a facility far away from people's neighborhoods would presumably provide the benefits while allowing them to avoid the costs or risks. This is the basis of the NIMBY Syndrome.

This theory argues that if people oppose siting a facility in their communities, the costs or risks are too high relative to the benefits. Thus, it prescribes that successful siting requires economic compensation so that the net cost calculation is improved. In the language of the economic theory, the expected net costs to a person facing the prospect of having a facility located near him or her can be expressed as:

$$ENC = \sum_{i=1}^{n} P_i\, C_i - \sum_{j=1}^{q} P_j\, B_j - M$$

where

ENC = expected net costs to the person

P_i = the person's estimate of the probability that the cost of impact i will be imposed on him or her

C_i = the cost of impact i to the person

P_j = the person's estimate of the probability that benefit j will be provided to him or her

B_j = the value of benefit j to the person

M = any monetary compensation the person receives

n = the number of impacts on the person

q = the number of benefits provided to the person

Clearly, according to this equation, expected net costs can be reduced by increasing monetary compensation. This suggests that in practice all that needs to be done is the level of M has to be set at a point which produces the desired expected net costs. As we noted in Chapter 1, this does not seem to have been successfully accomplished anywhere with respect to hazardous waste treatment facilities. However, this has led some analysts to try to derive rather precise estimates of the actual costs and benefits associated with a hazardous waste treatment facility (Smith, Lynn, Andrews, Olin, and Maurer, 1985). This seems to be motivated by the assumption that if public policy were to bring the level of compensation into line with the actual costs, public opposition would decrease. According to Lave and Romer (1983), developing workable compensation mechanisms would lessen the dissatisfaction of strongly dissatisfied groups.

Nowhere has this theory found a friendlier home than in Massachusetts. The initial Massachusetts siting law relied heavily on the theory of compensation, which prescribes that communities receive negotiated benefits in exchange for permission to site a facility (Portney, 1984). The state's 1980 Hazardous Waste Facility Siting Act became the statute establishing the outline of the process for locating hazardous waste treatment facilities in the state. According to the 1982 Statewide Environmental Impact Report issued by the Massachusetts Department of Environmental Management's Bureau of Solid Waste Disposal, the object of this law "is to assist the establishment of new, environmentally-sound hazardous waste facilities acceptable to all concerned parties—the host community, abutting communities, the developer, and the state"(Massachusetts Department of Environmental Management, 1982). The result of this process would ostensibly be "to reduce real and perceived risks, and to ensure that communities share in the benefits that the [hazardous waste] facility provides to the state." This would occur as a result of negotiations among the parties involved. Again, citing the 1982 Statewide Environmental Impact Report, "the key to a successful siting process is negotiation of the Siting Agreement between the developer and [the Local Assessment Committee of] the host community."

This approaches' appeal in practice comes from the idea that the state, a developer, and the people of a local community can all benefit from facility siting. The approach attempts, in practice, to produce a positive-sum result (Hansen, 1984). The idea is that lay perceptions of risk can and will be balanced by providing an opportunity to allow the benefits to exceed the costs implied by perceived risk.

Although this theory, and the processes prescribed by it, sound appealing, it seems fairly clear that it does not paint the whole picture. This is so because there is little evidence that it produces successful siting. First, no facilities have been successfully sited in Massachusetts. Second, states relying on compensation-based siting processes have experienced no greater success than those using other frameworks (Condron and Sipher, 1987). Third, there is very strong empirical evidence that people's net benefit calculations, to the extent that there may be such calculations, do not seem to be affected by increasing benefits at all.

Attempting to investigate the potential influences of changes in the benefits people receive from siting, the Citizen Survey Program at Tufts University conducted the two major survey research projects described in Chapter 1 to analyze residents' attitudes toward hazardous waste treatment facility siting. The first of these focuses on the potential for economic incentives in specific cities and towns (Portney, 1983; Portney, 1985). The Citizen Survey Program conducted in-depth interviews with over three-hundred randomly selected residents from each of five communities in the state. Brockton, Chelsea, Newton, Sturbridge, and Ware residents were chosen for this project.

We designed this survey to be community-based because the theory of compensation has implications for the way people in specific communities will react to economic incentives. Thus, we wanted to ensure that the results we obtained reflect an assessment of how the people in given communities respond.

The second project conducted by the Citizen Survey Program during 1984 consisted of interviews with over 500 citizens from a nationwide telephone survey. This survey focused on the contiguous forty-eight states and the District of Columbia. The main purpose of this study was to develop a base of comparison for the Massachusetts results and to begin an assessment of how generalizable the findings are.

Compensation and Public Attitudes
Survey Results

Our purpose in interviewing these residents was to develop a fairly clear picture of their benefit/risk calculations, if any, and to assess the potential for compensation in altering this calculation. Our method of trying to achieve this was to ask respondents first whether they would favor or oppose construction of a hazardous waste treatment facility somewhere in their state. Then, for those would said they favored or mostly favored such construction, we asked whether they would favor or oppose the siting of a hazardous waste treatment facility in their communities. Specifically, we asked:

A number of companies and the government have expressed the desire to build a hazardous waste treatment plant in (respondent's state). A hazardous waste treatment plant is a factory which tries to change hazardous waste into safe waste. A hazardous waste treatment plant does not bury wastes in any way. How would you feel about having such a plant built in your community. Would you say you favor having a company build a plant in (respondent's city or town), neither favor nor oppose it, oppose it or what?

In some instances, respondents initially answered that they had no opinion. For these people, we asked:

Would you say that you mostly favor or mostly oppose such a plant?

Overall in the Massachusetts survey, we found that nearly 62 percent of the people we interviewed opposed or mostly opposed facility siting in the state or in their neighborhoods. Table 2.1 presents a breakdown of how the five cities and towns and the nationwide sample differed with respect to opposing the construction of such a facility. These data suggest that each of the cities and towns starts in a somewhat different position in that the communities range in opposition from a little over half of the people (in Brockton) to over three-quarters (in Ware). In the nationwide sample, nearly 55 percent of the people opposed such a facility.

Respondents who opposed siting a facility in their city or town were asked to tell us how they would feel if various economic incentives were provided.[1] We focused on some nine economic incentive proposals which had been discussed in various siting negotiations in Massachusetts and which are expected to be linked directly to the benefit portion of people's personal calculus.

We also made an effort to ask people who opposed a facility to tell us how they would feel if measures were taken to decrease the risk portion of their calculus. We specifically focused on

Table 2.1
A Town-by-Town and National Summary of Respondents' Attitudes Toward Building a Hazardous Treatment Facility in Their Community

Sample	Respondents' Attitudes Toward Siting				
	Favor or mostly favor	Oppose or mostly oppose	Don't know	Total	n
Brockton	44.6%	54.2%	1.2%	100.0%	336
Chelsea	34.9%	55.9%	8.2%	100.0%	326
Newton	35.4%	62.3%	2.3%	100.0%	334
Sturbridge	20.8%	77.2%	2.0%	100.0%	303
Ware	22.8%	75.9%	1.3%	100.0%	316
Nation	17.8%	54.6%	27.6%	100.0%	564

safety precautions to get an idea of how much potential affecting the risk portion of the personal calculation might possess. The proposals we put to the respondents who said they opposed facility construction are summarized in Table 2.2. Here we can see the proposal, the problem immediately associated with facility construction, and the broader problem not necessarily associated with the facility, each proposal is designed to address. The first nine of these are economic incentive proposals, where the focus is on providing financial benefit or overcoming financial loss. The last two proposals are the proposals directed at alleviating peoples' fears or reducing people's assessment of high risks.[2]

Overall, in the Massachusetts samples, we found that some 43.9 percent of those who opposed or mostly opposed siting a facility in their community changed their minds under one or another of these eleven proposals. Nationally, we found that some 33.6 percent of such people changed their minds in response to at least one proposal. Table 2.3 provides a breakdown of the percentage of respondents initially opposing the facility who changed their minds under one or another of these proposals.[3]

Implications of the Survey Results

First of all, none of the proposals induces any sort of massive shift in public sentiment. The data in Table 2.4, which reflect the number of people who changed their minds as a percentage of the number of people who initially opposed the facility, show the basic patterns of change. While we would not necessarily expect people in every city or town to react identically to each proposal (because local conditions could well affect the marginal utility of various economic incentives), we do see remarkable similarity across communities. And the patterns are remarkably similar to those for the nation.

Perhaps the most useful way to examine the data in Table 2.4 is to compare the proposals within communities and to assess the relative rankings given to proposals across communities. We can also compare the ranking results from each city or town to those

Table 2.2
Eleven Proposals and the Immediate and Broad Problems Each Addresses

	Immediate Problem Addressed by the Proposal	Broader Problem Addressed by the Proposal
Economic Incentive Proposals		
1) Have the developer pay all property taxes for ten years.	The fear that the facility would increase the need for services, thereby increasing financial burden on the city or town.	Long-term increases in local property taxes
2) Have the developer pay a surcharge to the city or town based on the amount of waste processed.	Make company's payments to the city or town commensurate with the demands on the plant and surrounding community.	Again, long-term increases in local property taxes.
3) Have the developer hire at least 15 local local residents.	Fear that plant workers may not have sufficient stake in the effects of the plant on the community.	High unemployment.
4) Have the developer pay for improved fire protection.	Increased reliance on the local fire department to deal with the danger of explosion and accidental spills.	Fire department cuts brought about by a statewide property tax limitation passed in 1980.
5) Repave the city's streets.	Deterioration of streets because of heavy truck traffic around the facility.	Deterioration of streets because of statewide property tax limitation.
6) Have the developer provide five full college scholarships to local high school seniors each year.	Lack of local technical expertise to monitor plant operation.	Rapidly increasing costs of higher education.
7) $50 direct payment to each family in the city or town.	Residents' personal inconvenience and risk to personal property.	None

Table 2.2 (continued)

	Immediate Problem Addressed by the Proposal	Broader Problem Addressed by the Proposal
8) Have the developer pay the amount of any decrease in property values.	Decreases in the market values of homes because of proximity to the facility.	None
9) Have the developer purchase a life or health insurance policy.	Fear of risk of personal injury or loss from accidents not covered by existing insurance.	None
Risk Mitigating Proposals		
10) Have public officials and local citizens conduct regular safety inspections in the facility.	Low confidence in internal plant managements' dedication to safety over profit.	None
11) Have state and local officials do their best to prevent groundwater contamination and accidental spills.	Risk from contaminated water supplies and potential accidents.	None

Table 2.3
The Percentage of Respondents Initially Opposing the Facility Who Changed Their Minds Under One or Another Proposal, by Community and for the National Sample

	Responses to Proposals			
Sample	Percent Who Changed Their Minds to Favor	Percent Who Still Opposed	Total	n
Brockton	43.1%	56.9%	100.0%	336
Chelsea	46.4%	53.6%	100.0%	326
Newton	37.3%	62.7%	100.0%	334
Sturbridge	32.9%	67.1%	100.0%	303
Ware	56.4%	43.6%	100.0%	316
Nation	33.6%	66.4%	100.0%	564

Table 2.4
The Percentage of Respondents Opposing a Facility in Their Community Who Changed Their Minds in Response to Each of Eleven Proposals (Numbers in parentheses are rankings)

Proposals	Brockton n=336	Chelsea n=326	City, Town or Nation Newton n=334	Sturbridge n=303	Ware n=316	Nation n=564
Economic Incentive Proposals						
Pay all property taxes	7.5%(10)	10.5%(9)	10.2%(3)	5.6%(6)	17.9%(8)	5.3%(11)
Surcharge	12.0%(3)	11.4%(8)	10.2%(3)	9.4%(3)	16.6%(10)	9.2%(6)
Hire 15 local residents	11.3%(8)	12.2%(7)	7.4%(8)	4.7%(9)	25.9%(5)	9.9%(5)
Improved fire protection	12.8%(2)	13.8%(4)	9.1%(5)	4.7%(9)	26.2%(3)	12.2%(3)
Repave city streets	10.6%(9)	12.9%(6)	6.8%(9)	6.6%(5)	22.1%(7)	8.4%(7)
Five College Scholarships	12.1%(5)	15.4%(2)	5.7%(10)	9.4%(3)	24.8%(6)	6.9%(8)
$50 per family direct payment	6.0%(11)	7.3%(11)	5.7%(10)	2.8%(11)	15.2%(11)	6.9%(6)

Pay decreased property value	12.8%(2)	8.9%(10)	7.9%(7)	5.6%(6)	26.2%(3)	10.7%(4)
Buy health or life insurance policy	12.8%(2)	13.0%(5)	8.5%(6)	5.6%(6)	17.9%(8)	6.9%(8)

Risk Mitigating Proposals

Regular safety inspections	15.1%(1)	15.4%(2)	15.9%(1)	16.0%(1)	30.4%(2)	23.7%(1)
State and local efforts to prevent groundwater contamination and accidental spills	12.1%(5)	16.2%(1)	12.5%(2)	15.1%(2)	31.8%(1)	22.1%(2)

35

from the nationwide sample. Comparing the percentages them-selves across towns can be somewhat problematic. We see that in Ware, for example, all of the proposals changed a larger propor-tion of people's minds than in other communities. This is probably due to the fact that a relatively large proportion of people in Ware initially opposed the facility compared to the other communities. While the differences among the other communities seem much smaller, the interpretation of these percentages across communi-ties exhibits the same type of problem.

With this in mind, we can see that except in Brockton the risk mitigation proposals (safety inspection and prevention of ground-water contamination) seem to exert more influence on people's benefit/risk assessments than any of the economic incentives. Even in Brockton, the safety inspection proposal seems to have been the most influential among the proposals, although three of the economic incentives produced slightly greater change than the prevention of groundwater contamination proposal. This result for the nationwide sample is nearly the same. The pattern seems striking. Clearly, the risk mitigating proposals consistently produce greater changes of public sentiment than almost any economic incentive.

Variations on the Economic Compensation Theme

There are several theoretical variations on the compensation theme. To Kunreuther, Kleindorfer, Knez, and Yaksick (1987) the vehicle for compensation is a competitive bidding process in which several communities could submit to a developer sealed bids indicating how much compensation each would require in order to accept siting of a facility. The lowest bidder—the community asking for the least compensation—would be the "winner" and receive the facility. Developers proposing to build hazardous waste treatment facilities have in fact tried to create competitive bidding procedures, but frequently communities opt not to submit a bid at all because of the difficulty of designing a political process capable of defining what an acceptable bid would be. More recently, several companies have taken part in competitive bidding proposing benefits to a single community expressing a potential willingness and desire to accept a facility (Dabilis, 1989).

To Goetze, the major problem is that people have incentives to hide their true preferences, that is, they have incentives to say they want more compensation than they would actually accept. To him, the vehicle for overcoming the preference revelation problem is a choice of two types of insurance policies offered by the developer to residents in the prospective host community. In the first type of insurance policy, benefits would be paid to resident policy holders if a "hazardous contamination episode" occurs over some prescribed period of time. The second type of insurance would pay benefits to resident policy holders if such an episode *did not* occur over some period of time. Residents could choose which policy to acquire, but could not acquire both. In essence, people would be able to choose whether they want to bet that there will be an accident or bet that there will not be an accident.

However, it seems likely that unless there is some additional leverage brought to bear on residents of a potential host community, people will simply choose not to select either form of insurance, especially if they have to pay for it as envisioned by Goetze. Even if a developer offered to give such insurance to residents, it does not seem likely that most residents would be encouraged to stray from their original position of wanting to avoid facing the possibility of any accident. As we saw earlier, the promise of insurance by itself seems to change very few minds. It is difficult to understand why offering an alternative choice of an insurance policy which promises to pay benefits if no accidents occur would be any more effective in changing people's minds.

It is undoubtedly true that increasing benefits to individuals probably would at some point compensate for high costs. However, it seems that within the range of increased benefits that are possible in any facility siting situation, there is no way that the benefits can rise to that point. If any sort of change in the net calculation is possible, it seems that it can only occur as a result of decreases in the costs people *perceive* they must bear. Yet there is little evidence that there is any way to change people's perceptions about the magnitude of costs they must bear.

Perhaps the greatest problem with this set of prescriptions is its lack of empirical foundation establishing a causal link between increasing benefits and attitude change. When we found that people said they opposed facility siting because they were being asked to bear disproportionate costs relative to benefits, we began prescribing processes to allow benefits to increase. There is abundant evidence that this does not and will not work in practice (Portney, 1983; 1984; 1985; 1986; Elliott, 1985). One principal reason why these prescriptions do not and will not work is that they are built on faulty inferences about attitude change. The simple correlation between public articulation of high costs relative to benefits and attitudes opposed to facility siting does not establish a causal linkage between them. Moreover, it does not provide any information about the effects of changes in costs relative to benefits. We now know with 20/20 hindsight that the economic theory by itself will not provide sufficient prescriptions to permit successful treatment facility siting.

PUBLIC EDUCATION AND RISK COMMUNICATION

The Messages Sent Are Rarely the Messages Received

Since attempts to allow the benefits of siting to increase relative to costs was not particularly successful, in a sense attention turned to the cost portion of the calculation. For the most part, the costs that people were asked to bear are not tangible, but rather come in the form of high perceived risks to personal health and property. So our attention turned to ways of dealing with the perception of high costs in the form of high risks relative to benefits.

When we found that people said the risks were too high, we tried educating them to understand that the risks are not that high, especially when compared to the alternatives of using landfill technologies. Perhaps as much as anything else, this reflects a difference of opinion between "experts" and the general or "lay" public about how high the risks actually are (Fischhoff, Slovic, and Lichtenstein, 1983). It also seems to reflect a sense of frustration among experts at what they interpret (or misinterpret) as a public desire to make society "risk free"(Aharoni, 1981). The evidence is that such public education does little to alter people's perceptions of risk.

The current wisdom is that it is the risk communication process (usually thought of as the process by which experts communicate to non-experts the objective levels of risk) which is responsible, at least in part, for turning people against treatment facilities. The idea behind this is that when experts tell non-experts that the risks are really quite low, non-experts react to the communication process in a way that makes them conclude that the experts are wrong. This inevitably leads to prescriptions about how to improve the risk communication process as part of the overall management of risks (Thomas, 1986). In general, it leads us to search for modes of communication which will not be distrusted (Kasperson, 1986; Burger, 1984; Mazur, 1981). In particular, it implies that risk perceptions can and should be managed through some prescribed communication process or medium to allay people's fears. Risk communication has thus become synonymous with a decidedly one-way flow of information, from the experts to the general public, again directed toward the goal of changing people's attitudes. However, we should not be at all surprised if such prescriptions are no more successful than their predecessors. Indeed, given the fact that siting decisions will probably always engender media interest, there is plenty of reason to believe that changing risk communication processes can never fulfill this desired function (Mazur, 1989).

More recently, research has focused on assessing the extent to which public information programs are capable of actually changing people's perceptions of risk. Although there does not seem to be any such research focused on risk perceptions associated with hazardous waste treatment facility siting, there are several studies of changes in the perceived risks associated with exposure to radon (Smith, Kerry, and Johnson, 1988; Smith, Desvousges, Johnson, and Fisher, 1990). Specifically, Smith, Desvousges, Johnson, and Fisher have tried to determine whether the form in which information about radon is presented to people has an effect on the extent to which they find radon exposure to carry high or low risks. After initially measuring the extent to which people perceived risks to be associated with radon exposure, and after actually measuring the levels of radon in their respective homes, participants in this research were provided information about the levels of exposure to which they were actually exposed. Then, participants' risk perceptions were re-measured. Although they found some differences in the risk perceptions between the before and after comparison, generally people's perceptions of risk increased.

The perceptions of risk increased the most for people who initially perceived the risks to be least; and the perceptions increased the least for people who initially perceived the risks to be high. Although the authors interpret their results to mean that there are ways to modify people's perceptions of risk, the results of the analysis do not suggest ways that initially high perceptions can be diminished. Rather, the results simply suggest that the extent to which the perceptions increase may be affected by the form of the information presented to people. In other words, nearly everyone's perceptions increased with more information; the form of the information seems to have an influence on whether those perceptions increase a lot or a little.

More recently, analysis has turned its attention to more general issues of risk communication. In particular, the focus has become the processes actually used by people to communicate perceived risks. This has led to a more general understanding of the social processes through which risk information gets transmitted among people. Krimksy and Plough (1988) document, through a series of case studies of technical controversies, how complex the transmission of information is. Alluding to the difficulty of actually trying to control the risk communication process in given controversies, they suggest:

> Our studies demonstrate that under particular circumstances it is quite difficult for any single communicator to establish the boundaries of risk communication for an issue. . . .When there is a mix of conflicting messages, and an emotional issue . . . a communication process may result that is nearly impossible for any one communicator to control. (299)

The type of information found in Table 2.4 might lead us to believe that there is a causal relation between high perception of risk and opposition. Even if this relationship can be said to approach being causal, as we will argue it does in Chapter 4, it requires a major leap of faith to infer that changing the risk communication process will produce, or is capable of producing, a change in this relationship. It may be quite true that the messages sent from experts in commonly practiced risk communication media are not the messages received by non-experts. But this tells us little about the potential impact of altering the risk communication process. Even if the messages received are identical to the messages sent there is very little reason to believe that basic attitudes toward facility siting will change.

ENVIRONMENTAL NEGOTIATION AND MEDIATION

The Promise of Compromise and the Clash of Positions

The clash of opinion over where to site hazardous waste treatment facilities has not been ignored by the professionals who specialize in aiding the resolution of disputes. Increasingly, mediation and negotiation experts have brought their skills and experiences to bear on environmental disputes. Additionally, at least nineteen states make statutory or regulatory provision for incorporating negotiation or mediation opportunities into the siting process (Condron and Sipher, 1983: 16–17).

Typically, negotiation and mediation processes start with efforts by a neutral party, a negotiator or mediator, to "bring the parties together" in order to find some common ground for dispute resolution. It often attempts to help disputing parties reach some compromise so that to the extent possible each party's gains do not come at the expense of others. Mediation and negotiation processes often focus on converting what might initially be viewed as a "zero-sum" decision (where one party wins at the expense of others) into a "positive-sum" decision (in which everyone theoretically wins) (Talbot, 1983). Negotiation and mediation strategies have recently turned their attention to resolution of various scientific disputes. In some instances, they are proposed as expert-lay analogs to "scientific court" decision processes proposed for resolving disputes among expert scientists. Applications to hazardous waste treatment facility siting provide a specific scientific dispute in need of resolution.

The task confronted by mediation and negotiation specialists as applied to hazardous waste treatment facility siting is no easy one. Such an effort typically concentrates on a local decision where a developer wants to site a facility, the local populace opposes the proposed siting, and state and local public officials take various positions in support of, in opposition to, or neutral toward siting. This would seem to be a difficult, if not impossible, conflict to mediate or negotiate because it seems inherently "zero-sum." The facility is either sited or it isn't. If it is sited, the local populace loses; if it is not sited, the developer loses. However, most processes of this type turn their attention to whether there might be ways that siting can be accomplished while addressing the concerns and needs of the local populace.

The success of any particular negotiation or mediation process is assumed, at least in part, to be a function of merely using the process. At the risk of oversimplifying the problem, it appears that negotiation and mediation are advocated as a result of the observation that most local siting disputes have no clear-cut decision process or forum. So negotiation and mediation attempts to address the siting dispute by simply providing a structured inter-personal forum where disparate views can be articulated.

Such a structured process or forum does not automatically lead to successful siting (Buckle and Buckle, 1986). Early experience with this type of application, however, suggests that the success of negotiation and mediation is reliant on the range of benefits that can be addressed, something which is usually specified in and constrained by law. For example, where a negotiation or mediation process is used and state law does not provide for economic compensation, failure of the process seems almost guaranteed (Condron and Sipher, 1987: 20–21). However, there have been some efforts to clarify and specify the substantive focus of such mediation efforts.

Perhaps the most notable analysis of this type of process applied to hazardous waste facility siting is that by Elliott (1984). This analysis is based on a gaming exercise conducted in two communities. The exercise focused on hypothetical proposals to site treatment facilities with different technologies and which, presumably, would engender different risk perceptions from residents. In each community, a small group of eighteen people was assembled. These eighteen people represented public officials, businesses, environmentalists, and landowners. His results indicate that peoples' perceptions of risk associated with treatment facility siting have as much to do with management issues as they do with the specific technology employed or chemicals processed in the facility. For example, people expressed serious concern over such issues as delineation of operational responsibilities, availability of information to residents, having a regular and dependable structure or process for dispute resolution between the facility operator and residents.

Elliott's conclusions lend support to the findings concerning the importance of safety-related issues reported here earlier. However, they also point to the very real challenge faced by mediation and negotiation processes. There seems to be nothing about such processes, per se, which will lead to successful siting. At best, negotiation and mediation can serve as a vehicle for successful siting when used in conjunction with other considerations. At worst, mediation and negotiation are incapable of contributing to resolution of the specific disputes at hand. Rather, such strategies are often only able to reveal the deep sources of public opposition. The real keys, if there are any, would seem to lie elsewhere. If negotiation and mediation are to be successful, some as yet unidentified intervening factor(s) would appear to hold the key.

WHY PROMISING THEORIES SELDOM PRODUCE EXPECTED RESULTS

Perhaps the principle reason why we pursue prescriptions which end up to be fruitless in practice is rooted in how we derive these prescriptions. In formulating new policy proposals or prescriptions we tend to rely very heavily on analyses which identify very casually observed empirical correlates of attitudes or behavior opposing facility siting. Once we identify such a correlate, we often leap directly to a prescription or series of prescriptions which will in theory negate that correlate. Yet the record, as described above, seems to indicate that the empirical correlates rarely provide us with useful prescriptive information. For example, much was made out of the correlation between the fact that facility siting attempts provided affected people with little in the way of benefits relative to costs and the fact that these people almost universally opposed the siting attempt. This led, in part, to the prescriptions derived from the economic theory of compensation which called for provision of increased benefits relative to costs. When increasing benefits did not produce much attitude change, attention turned to reducing high costs as reflected in perceived risk.

If the prescriptions derived from these simple correlations are to be effective, the correlations must be assumed to reflect a causal connection between the respective variables. In the case of the economic theories, changing people's opposition by changing the benefits or costs of siting can only occur if there is a causal connection between low benefits relative to costs and opposition. In the case of attempts to allay opposition by changing people's perceptions of the high risks involved, we would only expect such a change to occur if there is a causal connection between risk perception and opposition.

The fact is that there is surprisingly little evidence to support the causal inferences on which any of the prescriptions rely. Standard empirical social science methodology provides clear guidelines on the prerequisites for causal inference, and virtually none of the simple correlations used to derive policy prescriptions seems to satisfy these conditions. Simply stated, none of the simple correlations rules out possible spurious influences on public attitudes.

Despite this pattern of reliance on simple correlations, we continue to search for additional correlates and new prescriptions. The risk communication process focus, for example, is perhaps best thought of as part of a larger concern about the lack of trust in American political and social institutions. Although people do indeed seem to have a high level of distrust in those who would site and operate facilities, there is very little reason to believe that altering the risk communication process will intervene in any clearly delineated causal relationship. Therefore, there is a strong possibility that this too might not yield effective prescriptions. We will investigate this specific relationship more fully in Chapter 3.

Mediation and negotiation prescriptions seem driven by the observation that the typical siting attempt lacks a clear decision process. The idea is that by carefully providing a neutral decision process (represented in mediation) where none existed before, a consensus can be reached. Again, the simple correspondence between the lack of a decision process and failure of siting leads some to prescribe creation of a decision process as the answer. Yet as we have seen, there is not a great deal of support for the idea that such a negotiation and mediation process, by itself, plays much of a role in successfully changing people's attitudes about siting. This is obviously why such strategies have turned their attention to understanding whether there are patterns to the substantive issues that tend to arise in negotiation and mediation efforts. This is not to say that the decision process is unimportant. Indeed, we will examine the importance of some additional elements of the decision process in Chapter 3. Suffice it to say that changing the inter-personal decision process provides us with only a portion of the puzzle we are trying to assemble.

THE PUBLIC POLICY DILEMMA AND EXPERIENCE: A SUMMARY

Not only do policy makers feel the need to search for ways of siting facilities to treat and dispose of hazardous wastes, they also feel intense pressure to preclude practically every specific site that can be selected. The result is that we simultaneously recognize the need to site treatment facilities while we realize that doing so appears to be nearly impossible. Many of the proposals formulated to assist the implementation of treatment-based hazardous waste policy seem not to offer generalizable answers.

Many of the proposals for allaying people's fears do not seem to have the desired effect. Instead, opposition to facility siting seems to remain rather consistently high or to actually increase as efforts to select specific sites progress. Attempts to redress imbalances in the costs and benefits of specific sites to affected residents have not made much difference. Environmental education programs aimed at changing people's perceptions of the relative risks of hazardous waste treatment facilities seem to have little or no effect in reducing public opposition. Even in experimental research on other environmental issues, there is very little evidence that public education programs are in any way capable of reducing people's perceptions of risk. There is evidence that information which does reach members of the general public has the effect of increasing people's perceptions of risks. Mediation and negotiation strategies, while still promising in general, have had only spotty success in affecting public opposition. Until we know with much more precision what kinds of substantive points tend to be most and least effective, it does not seem likely that mediation and negotiation strategies per se, will provide resolution to siting disagreements.

Perhaps equally as important as the relative ineffectiveness of various siting techniques is the fact that many such techniques are based on faulty, albeit sometimes ill-stated, assumptions about the roots of public opposition. Each siting intervention technique seems to be focused on a specific type of impediment to siting. Unfortunately, there is little or no evidence that any of these impediments actually causes public opposition. Indeed, if anything, the evidence suggests that while these techniques may work well in theory or in the abstract, they produce only the most disappointing results in terms of successful siting.

What is missing from this, in part, is a recognition that the siting process, especially the process whereby residents are able to block their community from being selected as a treatment facility site, is inherently political. Yet much attention has been paid to the idea that reforming the political processes, through which sites are selected holds the answer to successful siting. It is to this set of issues that we will turn our attention in Chapter 3.

NOTES

1. This, of course, presents respondents with a purely hypothetical situation upon which they must speculate. Although some respondents may act differently if actually faced with such a facility siting attempt, these data are clearly better than any other available information on the subject in that they provide us with responses to specific questions never before asked of people.

2. We rotated the presentation of these proposals to respondents to attempt to neutralize the possible influences exerted by question order on responses.

3. Obviously, this is a multiple response question set, so that the percentages of people changing their minds under the specific proposals reported later do not necessarily sum to the total percentage of people who changed their minds.

Chapter 3

The Politics of Siting: A Dilemma of Democracy in State and Local Efforts

Clearly the reform approaches discussed in Chapter 2, based on economic theories of compensation, conflict mediation and negotiation, and altering the risk communication process, have not produced the intended result. While it may not be particularly surprising that these approaches have met with such little success, it is curious how few reforms take into consideration that the siting process is inherently political. Yet when we examine the record of what our state and local governments have done in the effort to address hazardous waste treatment facility siting problems, there are some fairly clear notions of what should and can be done. Starting with state legislation to enable local treatment siting efforts, we will see that there is a variety of sentiment about how the process should and can work. However, we will also see that just as the more apolitical reforms were based on erroneous inferences, so too are the attempts to deal with siting as a political process.

STATE SITING LEGISLATION AS FLAWED POLITICAL PRESCRIPTIONS

In Chapter 1 we briefly reviewed some of the various approaches reflected in state legislation enabling the local siting of treatment facilities. We suggested that these could be categorized as representing the "pre-emption of local authority," the "state authority with local input," and the "primacy of local authority" approaches.

Each of these approaches can be thought of as constituting a very different statement about who should participate in the process, what implicitly constitutes an interest, and whose interests should be protected or potentially sacrificed. In the approach pursued by New Jersey, for example, the implication is that local interests should not necessarily be protected. In some instances, this idea of state pre-emption of local interests assumes a relationship between the form of democratic decision process and the resulting policy decision. There is a clear implication that hazardous waste treatment facility siting will be successful only if local interests can be sacrificed. In terms of democratic decision processes, this implies that the decision to be made is necessarily a zero-sum one, where it is inevitable that someone will lose in order for others to win. In order to accomplish this, some form of what is often called *adversary* democracy must be prescribed. In this case, the process would have to be defined such that the local needs or preferences of a specific community are not considered legitimate political interests.

On the other hand, approaches pursued, for example, by Florida imply that local interests should be protected. In still other states wishing to attempt to strike a balance, such as Massachusetts, the implication is that local interests should be protected within constraints. The constraints on protection of local interests often take the form of prescriptions about permissible decision-making processes. In Massachusetts, for example, state legislation carries a clear statement of how local citizen participation can take place. The different prescriptions about how local citizen participation can take place, however, often give way in practice to problems of implementation.

By now it seems to be fairly clear that state pre-emption of local interests constitutes something of a "myth"(Morell and Magorian, 1982; Hadden, Veillette, and Brandt, 1983). In other words, states in which local interests are potentially sacrificable have not had that experience in practice. The political reality seems to be that it is very difficult, if not impossible, to pre-empt local authority in practice. Moreover, pre-emption seems to be increasingly difficult to justify, given its obvious anti-democratic foundation.

Perhaps the more germane point is that the state policy makers who formulated and adopted these approaches seem to have fallen victim to the same type of flawed response as did their apolitical counterparts discussed in Chapter 2. Here the sequence starts with a recognition that "local" interests prevent siting, so the political response was to try to exclude local interests from the process. This exclusion of local interests from the formal process did not work, so efforts were made to include local interests but only in ways that would minimize the influence exercised by specific localities. In states such as New Jersey, there is an attempt to give local interests "representation" on a statewide siting board, but no particular local interest would be represented. The idea is that anyone serving as a representative of local points of view would be expected to show no favoritism toward his or her own community. This, however, has had no greater success than other approaches. Specific local communities still have been able to exercise their local influence to block treatment facility siting.

Yielding to the political belief that pre-emption of local interests does not work, states have embarked on a variety of ways to define processes where local interests are recognized. For the most part, it would seem that states wish to do this in ways that do not guarantee a negative result, that is, that do not automatically preclude successful siting. Many of these processes have taken on a decidedly more democratic tone, often calling for increased public participation in the process. If excluding intensely felt interests did not work, then perhaps advocating inclusion of these interests will lead to diminished opposition. In a sense, this is the same logic that influenced federal policy on nuclear waste disposal siting to prescribe state involvement in the site selection process (Downey, 1985). As a prescription for diminishing opposition, this, however, suffers from errors of inference about the causes of local public opposition that are not unlike those we have seen before. In order to begin to see how some would expect greater participation to reduce political conflict and why this will probably not happen, we must turn to what I call the "dilemma of democracy."

THE STATE POLICY PROBLEM AS A DILEMMA OF DEMOCRACY

There are many inherent problems with making public sector decisions involving risks. Sometimes, the major problem is that citizens have incentives to disguise their true preferences from decision makers. At other times, the problem is that it is difficult (or even impossible) for democratic institutions to be very unambiguous or specific about the goals associated with risky actions or events (Lave and Romer, 1983). But perhaps the most compelling major dilemma facing the siting of hazardous waste treatment facilities as a policy problem is what I call the "dilemma of democracy." Pursuing any policy response to hazardous waste problems must be the result of some democratic policy-making process. Knowing this, however, does not take us very far because the process can, and often does, unfold in various ways, all of which would still be considered democratic.

In perhaps the best analysis of the implications of relying on different democratic forms is found in the application of conceptual distinctions made by Mansbridge (1980) and applied to problems of hazardous waste facility siting by Matheny and Williams (1985). Mansbridge argues that much of what we believe to be democratic is of the "adversary" form, which is characterized by electoral representation, majority rule, and one citizen/one vote. This form of democracy assumes that citizens' interests are in constant conflict and that the democratic process must provide rules by which such conflicts can be resolved. Yet, according to Mansbridge, this adversary form contradicts what she calls "an older understanding of democracy." As she suggests:

In that older understanding, people who disagree do not vote; they reason together until they agree on the best answer. Nor do they elect representatives to reason for them. They come together with their friends to find agreement. (3)

Mansbridge argues that under the older form of democracy, there is an implicit assumption that ultimately citizens have a single common interest. For this reason, she refers to this as "unitary" democracy. Unitary democracy advocates a decision-making process in which disagreeing interests might work together to find some mutually agreeable decision. It stresses the possibility of obtaining a decision in which everyone can be said to benefit rather than a decision, as implied in adversary democracy, in which some interests are sacrificed for others.

Matheny and Williams suggest that we can see very clear reflections of each of Mansbridge's democratic forms in the different state and local approaches for responding to the hazardous waste problem. Each approach seems to make assumptions about the nature of conflict at the local level. Consequently, each prescribes a somewhat different way of resolving this conflict, leading presumably to successful hazardous waste treatment facility siting.

Matheny and Williams argue that elements of both adversary and unitary democracy must be present in successful siting processes. Elements of adversary democracy are necessary to deal with what they call the "redistributive aspects" of siting, that is, deciding who will get the site in his/her backyard so that everyone else can accrue the facility's benefits. Yet most processes do not account for potential political disagreement over the legitimate operation of the facility once sited. This, Matheny and Williams argue, must be addressed through unitary democratic processes.

There are two basic keys to successfully creating unitary democratic processes related to hazardous waste treatment facility operation. The first is the creation of a process which emphasizes structures for community control of the operation of any sited facility. The second is that strong measures need to be taken to convince affected local residents that they indeed have a shared interest in successful siting and facility operation. Matheny and Williams suggest that these two keys affect what they refer to as "second-stage legitimacy," or the legitimacy that people attach to the way the facility is operated.

Public Participation as the Solution

Much of the Matheny and Williams argument rests on the notions developed by Mansbridge and others concerning the relationship between participation in the political process and acceptance of that process as legitimate. Simply stated, as people having a shared or common interest participate in the process they develop a sense of legitimacy about that process and its results. For example, in interpreting the results of Elliott's (1984) siting simulation (which we reviewed briefly in Chapter 2) with respect to concerns about plant operation, Matheny and Williams state that:

> [The Elliott finding] indicates to us that second-stage legit-
> imacy in hazardous waste disposal facility siting is largely a
> matter of community *participation* in management rather
> than the *delegation* of management to experts. (77)

Indeed, this is a theme which has been developed in various ways by others (Kasperson, 1986; Ingram and Ullery, 1977; Davis, 1986; Rosenbaum, 1983; Kraft and Kraut, 1985). Increasingly, the "new wave" prescription for dealing with public opposition relies on some form of public participation in one or more stages of the siting process. Indeed, such prescriptions have even emerged from those who heretofore have engaged in the "professional" and scientific analysis of risk as divorced from analysis of public opposition. Even those who advocate relying on some type of compensation mechanisms admit that public participation processes are necessary, although participation usually means nothing more than voting on preferred levels of compensation (Kunreuther, Kleindorfer, Knez, and Yaksick, 1987: 382). Others seem to envision a more dynamic democratic process. For example, in an address at the 1986 annual meeting of the Society for Risk Analysis, Otway (1986) argued clearly that public participation holds the key to successful risk analysis and ultimately to successful resolution of scientific controversies which affect the public. As he notes:

> Controversy of itself is not necessarily bad; what we are seeing in most cases is simply democracy at work, but working poorly if all involved do not recognize the legitimacy of the process and the right of each to participate. Since risk analysis first emerged in response to controversy, and our main focus is on risks to the public, we should have something to offer. I think we do, but not by developing yet more rational methods of analysis (heaven knows, we have enough of them already), but rather by helping to make these processes more democratic and, thus, more effective.

At the risk of oversimplifying what is obviously a complex process, we can nevertheless try to depict the sequence of causal elements implied by the Matheny and Williams and related arguments with the following diagram:

Increased awareness of the need for treatment facilities $\xrightarrow{\ +\ }$ Sense of shared interest in facility operation $\xrightarrow{\ +\ }$ Acceptance of the decision to site and operate the facility in neighborhood

Participation or opportunity to participate in the process of plant operation $\xrightarrow{\ +\ }$ Sense of legitimacy about the decision process used $\xrightarrow{\ +\ }$

According to this argument, people must simultaneously develop a perception that they have a shared interest in the siting of a hazardous waste facility somewhere near their neighborhood and a sense of legitimacy about the process used to make the decision about how to operate the facility. Legitimacy is, at least in large part, a product of the opportunity to participate in the process of operating the facility. The perception of a shared interest has been thwarted in recent years by a growing distrust of the institutions or parties seeking to site facilities (Kasperson, 1986; Greenberg and Anderson, 1984). Overcoming this is largely the product of public education to increase people's awareness of the hazardous waste disposal problems as they currently exist.

We have argued elsewhere (Portney, 1990) that while these ideas about participation in siting processes are very much consistent with ideas expounded by democratic political thinkers from John Stuart Mill to Benjamin Barber concerning the ability of democratic systems to "build capacity" for responsible self-governance. Although we could not hope to do this general argument justice here, the idea is that when people participate in their own governance, they become better at it over time. In going through the process of self-governance, people are eventually exposed to the range of implications of their decisions and become increasingly capable of making decisions which presumably are based on more than short-term self-interest. Yet, even as described by advocates of more democratic forms, such participation must take place over much longer periods of time. New participants might make what turn out in the long run to be bad decisions. But as participants gain experience and exposure to making decisions, the decisions they make begin to address long-term considerations.

We can now see the potential problem with the earlier argument concerning participation: it is that, in the short run, the relationship between people's approval or sense of legitimacy of a given decision process and the results that the process produces often work in the opposite direction. In other words, the causation works in the other direction. This may be an especial problem in the case of siting hazardous waste treatment and other noxious facilities, where participation consists of attending hastily called public hearings and often attracts the participation of many people who may never have participated in anything more than voting. In such processes, people do not automatically accept a process as legitimate just because they participate, or are offered the opportunity to participate, in it. To a large degree, although certainly not universally, people will often deny the legitimacy of any process that produces a decision to site a facility where they do not want it. To many people, participation is legitimate because it provides them with an opportunity to obtain the results they want, namely preventing siting. To the extent that this is true, and to the extent that legitimacy is a prerequisite to siting, this is *the* major dilemma that has to be confronted before siting can be successfully pursued.

Some Empirical Foundations of the Dilemma

We are still left with the dilemma of democracy, described earlier. There are numerous empirical pieces that lead to an inference that such a dilemma of democracy does exist. Initially, Massachusetts provides a good case in point. Starting in the late 1970's, the state embarked on a two-pronged policy which conforms almost perfectly to that advocated by Matheny and Williams. First, a major media campaign was launched in order to convince people that treatment facilities were necessary. The media campaign was designed with the aid of substantial public opinion analysis. For example, television and radio announcements were made with personalities identified in public surveys as "highly trusted." Second, the state enacted a siting law, which we examined briefly in Chapter 2, designed to allow movement toward a unitary democracy approach.

It seems fairly clear that the siting approach advocated in this law intends to come fairly close to structuring unitary democracy in practice. Not only does the statute mandate local participation through the Local Assessment Committees (LACs), but it sets no limits on the items to be negotiated. The LACs can negotiate for substantial public participation in the operation of the facility if that is desired (Bacow and Milkey, 1982). Despite meeting the major requisites of the process advocated by Matheny and Williams, the Massachusetts law has been no more successful than any other law in setting in motion a political process leading to facility siting. To date, no facilities have been sited.

We would like to argue here that the reason for this relates to the dilemma we outlined earlier. In Massachusetts, the dilemma manifests itself in a particular way. Yielding to the argument made by people interested in ensuring that the 1980 siting bill would not pre-empt local interest, the legislature included a provision permitting state resources to be used by the LACs to support their efforts. The pro-local interests argued that in the absence of providing state resources, the bill's effect would be to overwhelm the resources that could be generated by almost any community, thus effectively pre-empting local interests. The message that came across was that any state-mandated process that did not provide resources to LACs would be suspect and perceived as illegitimate. However, the effect of having the state provide such resources was to give LACs what they needed to structure processes guaranteed to preclude siting in any specific city or town.

In addition to evidence from these state-sponsored siting processes, there have been a variety of experiments and pilot projects conducted with different systems for reaching or building consensus between developers and local interests. Some of these have involved intervention by mediation and conflict resolution experts (Talbot, 1983). Many states incorporate formal negotiation or mediation processes in statutes or regulations, while others strongly encourage such processes (Condron and Sipher, 1987:16–17). For the most part, the record indicates that pursuing a unitary approach to facility siting by involving citizens at an early stage is successful in creating a legitimate process only when siting does not occur.

The obvious prescription often derived from the "process legitimacy—opposition to treatment facility siting" relationship is to begin rebuilding trust. Indeed, this is the idea underlying much of the risk communication and mediation approaches discussed in Chapter 2. It is perhaps best thought of as part of a larger concern about the lack of trust in American political and social institutions, and a credibility gap between citizens and the officials these institutions represent (Greenberg and Anderson, 1984). Some have argued that what is missing here is a sense of trust in those who are to site and operate the facility (Kasperson, 1986; Elliott, 1984). If only people trusted their public officials, or the experts, or private companies, so the argument goes, then their perceptions of a clear health threat could be changed. Yet the fact is that general levels of "trust in American political and social institutions" have been declining for some time (Lipset and Schneider, 1983). Perhaps more importantly, empirical studies of trust in public institutions represented by their respective levels of government, such as the federal, state, or local government, have not been particularly successful in providing evidence on what its root causes are (Lipset and Schneider, 1983; Fischer, 1984; Baldassare, 1985).

Moreover, although people do indeed seem to have a high level of distrust in those who would site and operate facilities, there is a strong possibility that this too might not yield effective prescriptions. Even if we could infer something of a causal relationship, any specific intervention may not work. Indeed, there is no known way to rebuild trust in political and social institutions.

To demonstrate this, we can look at some data from the nationwide survey research project. In this survey, some 564 citizens were interviewed and queried about their attitudes toward hazardous waste treatment facility siting in their communities, as reported in Chapter 2. In this survey, we also asked people to tell us whom they would trust, if anyone, to build such a facility. Specifically, we asked:

If a hazardous waste treatment plant were built in your neighborhood, whom would you trust most to run it safely? Would you trust a private company, the state government, or the federal government to run such a plant safely?

We found, as shown in Table 3.1, that there was considerable variation in how people responded. We found that people tend to be almost evenly split among those who most trust private companies, the federal government, and their state governments to build and operate a facility. Almost eight percent said they would trust no one.

Table 3.1
Distribution of Respondents According to Which Institution They Most Trust to Build Hazardous Waste Treatment Facilities*

Most Trusted Institution	Percent of Respondents	Number of cases
None; trust no one	7.8%	43
Trust local officials	0.4%	2
Trust private companies	23.0%	130
Trust state government	21.6%	122
Trust federal government	24.8%	140
Trust federal and state governments together	5.3%	30
Trust "scientists," "citizen groups," or health professionals	3.6%	20
Don't know, can't say	13.8%	77
Total	100.0%	564

* *Question wording*: If a hazardous waste treatment plant were built in your neighborhood, whom would you trust more to run it safely. Would you trust a private company, the state government, or the federal government to run such a plant safely? (Other responses were volunteered).

The type of trust that people attach to different institutions appears to take on its importance if we examine its relation to facility siting opposition. Simply dividing people into those who oppose and those who do not oppose (as shown in Table 3.2), we can see that those who trust the federal government seem to be slightly less likely to be opposers than people who say they most trust other institutions. We might be led to infer from this that changing people's trust in the federal government would yield a reduction in opposition.

The fact is, however, that the vast majority of people who say they most trust any institution, or no institution at all, oppose siting. Moreover, people who said they most trust their state governments are actually slightly more likely to oppose facility siting than those who trust no one. Thus, there is at least some reason to believe there may not be much correlation between specific levels of trust and opposition.

The potential lack of correlation gives us *prima facie* evidence that attempts to rebuild trust may not work. There is some additional evidence on this point. If we look at the extent to which people seem to be willing to change their opposition in response to proposals designed to meet their concerns, trust does not seem to play a major role. (For a more detailed examination of the issue of "change" in attitude toward facility siting, see Chapter 5.) Table 3.3 shows, for example, that when offered guaranteed safety inspections by local citizens and officials (surely a component of what Matheny and Williams call the "second-stage" of the siting process), people who say they most trust the federal government are not more likely than people who trust other institutions to drop their opposition. Indeed, if trust in any one institution intervenes in the relationship and siting, it is trust in the private sector. Of those people who most trust the private sector, more than four out of ten indicated that they would be satisfied to drop their opposition if local citizens and officials were involved in safety inspections. Most people, however, do not change their minds regardless of which institution, if any, they most trust.

Table 3.2
The Relationship Between Trust and Opposition to Hazardous Waste Treatment Facility Siting in Respondent's Community*

Most Trusted Institution	Attitude Toward Treatment Facility		
	Oppose	Don't Oppose	Total
None; trust no one	72.7%	27.3%	100.0%
Trust local officials	0.0%	100.0%	100.0%
Trust private companies	67.7%	33.3%	100.0%
Trust state government	78.7%	21.3%	100.0%
Trust federal government	64.3%	35.7%	100.0%
Trust federal and state governments together	66.7%	33.3%	100.0%
Trust "scientists," "citizen groups,"or health professionals	50.0%	50.0%	100.0%

* *Question wording*: "A number of companies and the government have expressed the desire to build a hazardous waste treatment plant in [respondent's state]. A hazardous waste treatment plant is a factory which tries to change hazardous waste into safe waste. A hazardous waste treatment plant does not bury wastes in any way. Would you say you would favor having a company build a plant in your community, neither favor nor oppose it, oppose it, or what?" Those who responded "neither" or "don't know" were asked "Would you say you mostly favor or mostly oppose such a plant?"

Table 3.4 shows the same sort of pattern, this time considering the role that trust plays when groundwater protection practices are built into the operation of the facility. Again, trust in the private sector seems to be slightly more capable of getting people to change their minds if a serious effort is made to protect nearby groundwater. But most people still oppose the facility regardless of whom they most trust.

It seems clear, at least from the very basic data presented here, that there must still be something that makes people's opposition to hazardous waste facility siting so strong. Trust in political and

Table 3.3
The Relationship Between Trust and Change in Opposition in Response to a Promise of Local Citizens and Official Involvement in Plant Inspections*

Most Trusted Institution	Change in Attitude Toward Facility**		
	Still Opposed	Not Opposed	Total
None; trust no one	95.0%	5.0%	100.0%
Trust local officials	a	a	a
Trust private companies	58.9%	41.1%	100.0%
Trust state government	67.3%	32.7%	100.0%
Trust federal government	68.5%	31.5%	100.0%
Trust federal and state governments together	84.6%	15.4%	100.0%
Trust "scientists," "citizen groups," or health professionals	75.0% 80.0%	25.0% 20.0%	100.0% 100.0%

* *Question wording*: "A number of different proposals have been made by companies and the government to address peoples' worries. I would like to read you a list of some of these. After I read each one, please tell me how you would feel about building a hazardous waste treatment plant in your neighborhood if this and only this is done: If the company offered a guarantee of a regular safety inspection by city or town residents and officials, would you favor, neither favor nor oppose, or oppose the plant?"

** As a percentage of respondents who initially said they were "opposed" as reflected in Table 3.2.

a None of the respondents who said they most trusted local officials opposed the siting, as reflected in Table 3.2. Therefore, there was no basis for calculating change in opposition here.

social institutions may play a role in this opposition, but it seems more likely that this is another symptom of an attitudinal process that we have only begun to understand. Our efforts in Chapters 4 and 5 will be directed toward an examination of some of the

Siting Hazardous Waste Treatment Facilities

Table 3.4
The Relationship Between Trust and Change in Opposition in Response to a Promise of Efforts to Prevent Groundwater Contamination*

	Change in Attitude Toward Facility**		
Most Trusted Institution	Still Opposed	Not Opposed	Total
None; trust no one	95.0%	5.0%	100.0%
Trust local officials	a	a	a
Trust private companies	66.7%	33.3%	100.0%
Trust state government	68.5%	31.5%	100.0%
Trust federal government	87.8%	22.2%	100.0%
Trust federal and state governments together	92.3%	7.7%	100.0%
Trust "scientists," "citizen groups," or health professionals	100.0%	0.0%	100.0%

* *Question wording:* "What if state and local officials did their absolute best to prevent groundwater contamination and accidental spills?"
** As a percentage of respondents who initially said they were "opposed" as reflected in Table 3.2.
[a] None of the respondents who said they most trusted local officials opposed the siting, as reflected in Table 3.2. Therefore, there was no basis for calculating change in opposition here.

stronger correlates of local public opposition, and correlates of change in attitudes.

Now we can begin to see how the dilemma of democracy manifests itself. Simply stated, no known specific democratic procedure has yet been found which makes successful hazardous waste treatment facility siting likely, or even possible, in practice. Serious local citizen involvement in the siting process has been lacking, as has been a sense of legitimacy about the process itself. In the absence of process legitimacy, no siting can be successful. Yet increasing public involvement in the entire process does not necessarily produce a more legitimate process. If siting is successful, the process may still be considered illegitimate even in the face of participation. Thus, there is good reason to believe that it may be the *result* of the process that affects people's senses of how legitimate that process is. From the perspective of the interest in successful siting, citizen participation now seems absolutely necessary if the process is to be seen as legitimate. Yet increased participation goes a long way toward ensuring an unsuccessful siting process, precluding the promised effect of creating a legitimate process.

This is not to say that citizen involvement is unimportant. Citizen participation may well end up providing the only qualitative check on the actual management of treatment facilities. Although some may find it hard to accept, treatment facilities having substantial citizen participation in their operation may turn out to be much safer in the long run than those having none. The point here, however, is that citizen participation in siting, even when accompanied by promised citizen participation in management, is not likely to produce a more successful siting process. Indeed, greater citizen participation may preclude successful siting.

PUBLIC PARTICIPATION IN SITING WITHIN A DEMOCRATIC CONTEXT

To some, pursuing a policy which stimulates public involvement merely constitutes an extension of democracy in practice. It almost goes without saying that these proponents of participation in siting decisions value the tenets of self-governance. Democratic theory argues that there are very important positive benefits which purport to accrue as a result of popular governance, and it would be impossible to fully review such a theory here. It is clear, however, from the pro-participation works of Mansbridge and Barber, for example, that popular democracy should, in the long run, lead to greater popular understanding of problems and more responsible decisions. But to many participation proponents, participation is highly valued in and of itself, and the resulting decisions are responsible regardless of what they are. To such people, the issue is one of empowerment rather than making a particular decision (Hayes, 1984).

Ironically, popular participation in hazardous waste facility siting has led many people to the opposite conclusion. To those who have reached the opposite conclusion, the more people are involved the harder it is to site hazardous waste facilities. To them, it may be more democratic for people to participate, but participation is not a responsible part of the process if the facilities are prevented. To such people, this is an example of democracy rearing its ugly head (Edelstein, 1988: 171; MacDonald, 1984).

The problem this poses for democracy is over-simplified by both arguments. To many democratic thinkers, public participation is something that cannot take place in a sporadic fashion. Public participation pays dividends only when people become involved in face-to-face situations over a relatively long period of time. The idea is that as people get involved in more and more situations, they begin to understand the specific problems at hand and become increasingly willing to accept some form of compromise as a resolution. People who perhaps once participated while viewing a given decision as a zero-sum game become more willing to entertain positive-sum resolutions. In order to achieve this type of participation, however, people must be more generally involved in governance decisions.

When people do not participate by taking part in activities with more direct face-to-face contact than voting, they lose the sense that compromise is valuable and become less willing to entertain resolutions other than the ones they advocate. Thus, the political stalemate that is often associated with public participation in hazardous waste facility siting decisions is really a consequence of short-term participation by people who have not experienced the benefits of long-term commitments to participation. This may in fact be what explains what has been described as an unusually high potential for success reported in the California planning process associated with the Southern California Hazardous Waste

Management Authority (Mazmanian, Stanley-Jones, and Green, 1988). Here, siting is treated as part of a much longer-term and general environmental planning process where public participation has become an integral part of the process. However, even here, there has been no successful siting effort to date.

Even if regularized participation holds promise, the problem for hazardous waste facility siting in a democratic context is that most places around the country today do not have the benefit of deep, broad-based, regularized citizen participation. Thus, to stimulate short-term participation for the sole purpose of facility siting invites the danger of stimulating rather vocal and unyielding opposition. Unfortunately, proponents of treatment facility siting find themselves in the unenviable position of having to oppose seemingly democratic processes.

Indeed, there is some recent evidence that parties involved in trying to site facilities are increasingly turning to the SLAPP, or Strategic Lawsuit Against Public Participation, strategy in order to prevent public participation. SLAPP law suits are actions taken by siting parties in civil court against groups or individuals exercising what they believe to be their constitutional right to participate. The legal grounds on which these law suits are brought varies, but they always seek the same end: to deter public opposition to facility siting. Depending on how successful these law suits are, this strategy may make siting unpopular facilities a little easier in the short run, but they do little for promoting democratic ways of resolving conflict. If the earlier experience with efforts to limit public participation teach anything, they may suggest that this strategy will not be successful in the long run.

THE POLITICAL PROCESS AND LOCAL OPPOSITION: A SUMMARY

There have been a variety of attempts to exercise influence over the process of siting hazardous waste treatment facilities by affecting the political process. Earlier attempts at siting pursued the idea that local interests, which would naturally oppose and prevent siting, should be excluded from the process if siting was to have a chance of succeeding. Such exclusion, which took the form of pre-emption of local authority, simply did not happen in practice.

Subsequently, attention has shifted 180 degrees, advocating inclusionary processes in which affected local interests would play an explicit role in siting. Only through such participation, so the argument goes, would people begin to accept the process as legitimate and develop the levels of trust needed to site and operate a treatment facility. There is plenty of evidence to suggest that participatory processes might be effective, indeed might be needed, in order to build the kind of long-term trust and personal capacity to make facility siting possible. Yet, as envisioned to date, inclusionary approaches which focus only on short-term and sporadic participation are likely to meet with every bit as much difficulty as their exclusionary counterparts.

Recently, parties in siting efforts, turning to the courts for relief, have started to use the SLAPP approach. So we seem to be in the process of making another 180 degree turn. There is little reason to believe that limiting public participation through this mechanism will be any more successful in getting facilities sited than its predecessors.

So this is the dilemma of democracy. Unfortunately, understanding the roots of the dilemma by itself provides no guidance on how successful siting might occur. Before we can begin to seek such explicit guidance, we need to turn our attention to an assessment of what it is that seems to cause people to oppose siting in the first place. It is to this general topic that we turn our attention in Chapter 4.

Chapter 4

Correlates of Public Opposition: What We Know and Don't Know About the Influences on People's Attitudes Toward Treatment Facility Siting

Relying on simple correlates of public opposition for guidance, either through casual observation or through more systematic analysis, has sometimes led to misleading conclusions and useless prescriptions about changes in people's opposition to hazardous waste facilities. The task before us is to start with a somewhat more basic understanding of some of the major factors which seem to influence opposition and to assemble what we know and do not know about opposition and changes in this opposition in order to provide a clear foundation for public policy. In fact, because the level of public opposition has so frequently mistakenly been used as a proxy for examining changes in opposition, we know less than we might like to admit about the correlates of change. Much of what we can be said to know necessarily comes from inferences involving correlates of opposition. In the process of drawing out these inferences, we must take care to temper our conclusions depending on any anticipated spuriousness. We can start our investigation by examining the correlates of opposition, saving our analysis of the correlates of changes in opposition for Chapter 5.

Relying on correlates of opposition does not alter the fact that our main interest is in changing opposition to facility siting. Although the main focus of our effort is on understanding what decreases opposition, we probably know more about what increases people's opposition. Part of the reason for this is that there seems to be a general tendency for public opposition to be increasing over time. Nevertheless, we will make an attempt to summarize what we know about what, if anything, diminishes public opposition to facility siting.

In the previous chapters, we periodically focused on several more commonly identified specific correlates of public opposition, but we never assessed a fuller range of conceptual and empirical variables associated with that opposition. For example, in Chapter 3 we examined the linkage between "trust in government and sense of legitimacy about the siting process" and public opposition. Here, in order to develop a sense of how complicated, and perhaps how misunderstood, public opposition is, we review some of the empirical research on a fuller range of correlates of that opposition.

After we make an effort to review what we know and do not know, we will attempt to identify those areas in which more information and research is clearly needed. We will not try to draw out the public policy implications of the state of our current knowledge in this chapter. Rather, after we put this information into its social, psychological, and political contexts in Chapter 6, we will address the public policy implications in Chapter 7.

CAUSES AND CORRELATES

Although there does not seem to be any clearly identifiable body of research which relies on a causal framework, many studies have attempted to uncover correlates of, or factors associated with, public opposition. In most cases, analyses fall short of drawing causal inferences from their results, often because the results are not powerful enough to warrant such inferences. Nevertheless, much of this research leads us almost to the doorstep of inferring that there may be some causal relationship at work.

Of course, the reason that understanding the correlates of opposition is so important is that we would expect the patterns to permit us to make inferences about what, if anything, might be done in the way of changes in public policies to change that opposition. If we were to find, for example, that most of the people who exhibit the strongest opposition to facility siting are the least well educated in environmental issues, as some have suggested, then one possible inference we might draw from this is that opposition can be reduced by providing people with some basic knowledge and information about environmental issues. We will discuss some problems with relying on this type of inference later.

THE RELATION BETWEEN SOCIO-ECONOMIC STATUS AND OPPOSITION

The literature linking socio-economic status to environmentally related attitudes and behavior is somewhat ambiguous. When it comes to the expression of concern about the environment, there is apparently little connection with socio-economic status (Mohai, 1985:821). When it comes to being an active advocate of environmental protection, there does seem to be some relation with socio-economic status (Mohai, 1985; Buttel and Flinn, 1978a; Buttel and Flinn, 1978b). Whether socio-economic status can be said to influence attitudes toward siting hazardous waste treatment facilities is still an open question.

Based on analysis of concern about toxic wastes, it seems possible that income, education, and race may play significant roles (Hamilton, 1985a; Hamilton, 1985b). In the case of income, people with greater resources tend to live in areas where industrial activity is limited. Siting a hazardous waste treatment facility in such areas might be expected to stimulate significant opposition. The effects of education, defined as exposure to formal schooling, may be expected to parallel those of income. However, it has also been suggested that education, defined as specific knowledge about the environment, may be expected to work in the opposite direction. People who know very little about the environment may not understand the full implications of opposition to building treatment facilities. On the other hand, people who are aware of the threat from currently practiced hazardous waste disposal methods might be the people most likely to understand why it is important to site treatment facilities, and therefore be less opposed.

As we can see from Table 4.1, there is not a particularly strong relationship between family income[1] and attitude toward facility siting. In general, there is a tendency for people at all three income levels to oppose facility siting both anywhere in the state and in their own communities. High income respondents, however, reveal a slightly different profile from their lower income counterparts. Higher income people seem slightly less likely to not oppose facility siting in both the state and local community, instead tending to be more likely to exhibit NIMBY attitudes. The extent that there is any relationship between income and type of opposition is due to the modest tendency for higher income people to more likely be NIMBY Syndromers than lower and middle income people.

While we did not ask respondents about their formal education attainment, we did ask a short series of questions to estimate how much "environmental knowledge" each respondent possessed. To do this, we asked respondents to tell us whether each of five substances could be considered hazardous waste. The substances, gasoline, old lead paint, nuclear waste, used motor oil, and empty beer bottles, all possessed some degree of hazardous properties. However, we were most interested in whether people could make the major distinctions among types of dangerous materials.

We used the answers to these questions to assess respondents' respective environmental knowledge. Initially, we assessed each answer to determine whether it was correct, that is, whether the respondent accurately identified the hazardous waste materials as such. To do this, we had to make a decision about which of the five materials really could be considered a hazardous waste. Clearly, empty beer bottles are not of the same class of hazard as the other four substances. Initially, we intended to focus more on the legal definition of hazardous waste, which typically does not include nuclear waste. However, since nuclear waste is certainly

Table 4.1
The Relationship Between Family Income and Opposition to Hazardous Waste Facility Siting in Five Massachusetts Cities and Towns Combined

	Family Income		
	Low	Middle	High
Favor or mostly favor siting in state and local community	34.7%	35.1%	32.7%
Oppose or mostly oppose siting in both state and local community	42.8%	41.6%	37.1%
NIMBY – Favor or mostly favor in state but not in local community	22.5%	23.3%	30.2%
Total percent	100.0%	100.0%	100.0%
n	418	493	410

Pearson Chi-square = 8.34   Significance = .08

among the most lethal we examined, it made more sense to include this as a recognized hazardous material.

We used the answers to these questions in two ways. First, we simply counted how many of the five substances each respondent identified correctly. Second, we simply characterized each person according to whether he/she did or did not get them all correct. Then we correlated these levels of environmental knowledge with the type of attitude toward hazardous waste facility siting. These results are found in Tables 4.2 and 4.3.

In Table 4.2 we can see that the people who knew the absolute least (albeit only eighteen respondents) were less opposed to facility siting than any of their more knowledgeable counterparts. The table also reveals that general opposition to both state and local siting increases consistently as the level of knowledge increases *except* for the very most knowledgeable people. The people who correctly identified whether all five substances are

Table 4.2
The Relationship Between Level of Environmental Knowledge and Attitudes Toward Treatment Facility Siting in Five Massachusetts Cities and Towns Combined

| | Number of Hazardous Substances Correctly Identified | | | | | |
	0	1	2	3	4	5
Favor or mostly favor siting in state and local community	44.4%	34.4%	35.5%	32.8%	33.4%	30.6%
Oppose or mostly oppose siting in both state and local community	27.8%	39.1%	40.5%	40.7%	45.7%	38.5%
NIMBY - Favor or mostly favor in state but not in local community	27.8%	26.6%	24.0%	26.6%	20.9%	30.9%
Total percent	100.0%	100.0%	100.0%	100.0%	100.0%	100.0%
n	18	64	200	369	569	327

Pearson Chi-square = 14.64   Significance = .15

hazardous wastes were somewhat less likely than most of their less-knowledgeable counterparts to oppose siting in the state and in their respective communities. However, these people are clearly the most likely to be NIMBY-Syndromers. People who have the most environmental knowledge are among the most likely to see the need for a treatment facility somewhere in the state but simultaneously oppose such a facility in their communities. In terms of general opposition, there is modest support for the idea that a little knowledge can be dangerous. However, in terms of the NIMBY Syndrome, it seems fairly clear that a lot of knowledge can be dangerous.

This latter pattern can be seen more clearly in Table 4.3 where the independent variable from Table 4.2 has been dichotomized. Here we see that people who did not know all five substances were more likely than their more knowledgeable counterparts to express general opposition, while those who did know all five

Table 4.3
The Relationship Between High Level of Environmental Knowledge and Type of Attitude Toward Hazardous Waste Facility Siting in Five Massachusetts Cities and Towns Combined

	Level of Environmental Knowledge	
	Respondent did not get all five substances correct	Respondent got all five substances correct
Favor or mostly favor siting in state and local community	33.8%	30.6%
Oppose or mostly oppose siting in both state and local community	42.7%	38.5%
NIMBY – Favor or mostly favor in state but not in local community	23.5%	30.9%
Total percent	100.0%	100.0%
n	1220	327

Pearson Chi-square = 7.44   Significance = .02

were considerably more likely to favor building a facility somewhere in the state as long is it was not in their respective communities.

THE GENDER GAP: THE RELATIONSHIP BETWEEN GENDER AND OPPOSITION

One of the recurring themes found in environmental sociology is the gap between men and women with respect to concern for, and desire to improve, the physical environment. There have been a number of ways that this gender gap has manifested itself in existing research. Women have played a distinct role as environmental activists; have been shown to differ significantly from men with respect to willingness to live near, and general acceptance of, nuclear power generating plants; and have been found to be more supportive than men of public efforts to improve and protect the environment (McStay and Dunlap, 1983; Dunlap and Catton, 1979; Catton and Dunlap, 1978). This cannot be considered a generalized finding; indeed, numerous studies have failed to find gender differences, and some have found men to be more concerned than women (Van Liere and Dunlap, 1980; Arcury, Scollay, and Johnson, 1987).

The literature on environmental activism occasionally points to the implication that gender plays a significant role. Perhaps starting with recognition of the role played by Lois Gibbs in the Love Canal area of New York (Levine, 1982), it has been suggested that women's attitudes toward environmental issues are often considerably different from those of men. This gender-gap hypothesis, as it might be called, points clearly toward the suggestion that women are more risk-averse when it comes to living with or near environmental hazards, and may also exhibit general values that preclude the presence of such hazards anywhere.

The gender gap extends beyond a propensity to become involved in personally important issues. Perhaps starting in the mid-1970s public opinion research began discovering a fairly significant difference in the way men and women responded to the idea of relying on, and living near, nuclear power generating plants. Passino and Lounsbury (1976) reported substantial differences in levels of support and opposition for building nuclear plants, with men more supportive and women more opposed. Nealy, Melber, and Rankin (1983), as well as Passino and Lounsbury (1976) analyzed nationwide public opinion data from several sources and discovered that women were considerably less likely than men to support the use of nuclear power, and were even less supportive of the idea of having such a facility located near their communities. In a separate study, Brody (1984) also found that women were more opposed than men to general use and local siting of nuclear plants. George and Southwell (1986) verified that women were significantly more likely than men to oppose licensing of the Diablo Canyon nuclear power plant in California.

More recently, in an effort to clarify and better specify the relationship between gender and attitudes toward the environment, several studies have suggested that there are gender differences on some kinds of issues and not others. In particular, the implication is that gender differences exist on local environmental issues, especially those with health and safety dimensions (Passino and Lounsbury, 1976; Stout-Wiegand and Trent, 1983). Blocker and Eckberg (1989) have argued that there are gender differences when the issue becomes local, at which time women's attitudes become a reflection of their protective "motherhood" roles. This tends to support Hamilton's finding (1985a; 1985b) that mothers are more concerned about local toxic wastes than men or women without children.

Because of these rather consistent male-female differences on issues of the environment, at least with respect to nuclear power and local environmental issues, one might speculate that the pattern should hold for situations involving siting hazardous waste treatment facilities. Thus, we might expect women would be more likely than men to be opposed to hazardous waste treatment facility siting. Moreover, we would probably expect that women would be more likely than men to exhibit the NIMBY Syndrome, since this is the specific issue at hand which carries the strongest "local" connotations. This pattern is investigated in Table 4.4.

The relationship between gender and attitude toward facility siting is extremely strong. The major difference between the genders is that women tend to be much more opposed than are men to facility siting anywhere in the state. While over forty-one percent of the men we interviewed favor or mostly favor siting a treatment facility in their local communities, only about a quarter of the women expressed this attitude. On the other hand, while about a third of the men in our samples expressed general opposition to facility siting anywhere in the state, nearly half of the women were generally opposed. Men and women do not seem to differ at all with respect to the NIMBY Syndrome. Women are

Table 4.4
The Relationship Between Gender and Attitudes Toward Treatment Facility Siting in Five Massachusetts Cities and Towns Combined

	Gender of Respondent	
	Male	Female
Favor or mostly favor siting in state and local community	41.6%	25.5%
Oppose or mostly oppose siting in both state and local community	33.4%	49.4%
NIMBY - Favor or mostly favor in state but not in local community	25.0%	25.1%
Total percent	100.0%	100.0%
n	731	816

Pearson Chi-square = 53.8   Significance = .00

not more likely than men to exhibit local opposition only. Thus if there is a gender gap in attitudes toward facility siting, it is characterized by the fact that women simply do not accept as a given that treatment facilities are needed anywhere. Men, on the other hand, seem more likely to accept treatment facilities as necessary.

While the gender gap is extremely strong, it is not obvious why it should be so. We can investigate several different types of reasons why women are more inclined than men to generally oppose facility siting. One possible reason, as we suggested earlier, relates to the role of women as mothers (or potential mothers), nurturers, and protectors of children. One way of investigating this possibility is to look at whether women who have children in their respective households are more likely than men and women without children to oppose facility siting. This relationship is found in Table 4.5.

Table 4.5
The Relationship Between Women with Children and Opposition to Facility Siting in Five Massachusetts Cities and Towns Combined

| | Gender and child status | | | |
| | Women | | Men | |
Attitude Toward Siting	With Children	Without Children	With Children	Without Children
Favor or mostly favor siting in state and local community	27.7%	24.3%	38.8%	42.2%
Oppose or mostly oppose siting in both state and local community	49.1%	49.9%	37.2%	31.2%
NIMBY - Favor or mostly favor in state but not in local community	23.2%	25.8%	24.0%	26.6%
Total percent	100.0%	100.0%	100.0%	100.0%
n	346	449	304	448
Pearson Chi-square =	1.50		2.85	
Significance =	.47		.24	

Overall Pearson Chi-square = 53.85   Significance = .00

Here we see that gender, rather than having children, makes the greater difference. Women with children actually seem a little less opposed to facility siting than women without children. The pattern in Table 4.5 shows that half of the women, regardless of whether they have children in their households, oppose facility siting. And women, whether they have children or not, are considerably more likely to oppose siting than men, regardless of whether the men have children in their respective households. As was the case in Table 4.4, women, regardless of whether they have children, are not more likely than men to exhibit the NIMBY Syndrome.

Thus, the explanation that women are more opposed to facility siting than men because they are more concerned than men about the health and well-being of their children does not seem to be supported by these data. Indeed, the fact that women are not more likely than men to be NIMBY Syndromers opposed to local siting may be a reflection of this. These results do not appear to be particularly consistent with the idea put forth by Williams, Jobes, and Gilbert (1986:631) that the reason why there is a difference is that "women have been heavily socialized into expressive rather than instrumental roles and behavior, [and as a result] they are more likely to value noneconomic qualities than are men." If one of these roles is associated with child-bearing and rearing, then this does not appear to be a strong determinant of women's attitudes toward siting except under one or both of two conditions. First, the socialization process might take place equally strongly for women regardless of whether they actually have children, in which case actually having children would not necessarily make a difference. Second, women might understand the relationship between siting anywhere in the state and its local implications, opting to oppose the siting in principle because of its possible threat to their own communities. However, the data are perhaps more consistent with the notion that women tend to have different fundamental values with respect to the environment than do men (Catton and Dunlap, 1978; Dunlap and Catton, 1979; Merchant, 1980).

THE RELATIONSHIP BETWEEN COMMUNITY ROOTEDNESS AND OPPOSITION

It has been suggested that the more people are rooted in a given community, the more likely they are to oppose local facility siting (Edelstein and Wandersman, 1987). Indeed, we would probably expect that people who are rooted in a community by virtue of having made something of a financial investment in a home to be more protective of their communities than people who are less rooted by virtue of being renters. This expectation derives from the assumption that homeowners would have to bear greater costs and would find it more difficult to change residences than their renter counterparts. Thus, the assumption is that renters would be more likely not to oppose facility siting but would simply move.

In addition to home ownership as an indicator of community rootedness, we can look at how long people have lived in the community. People who have lived in a community for longer periods of time might be expected to have developed a greater sense of rootedness and, as a consequence, might also be less willing to see the community threatened by a hazardous waste treatment facility. These relationships are presented in Tables 4.6 and 4.7, respectively. In both cases, the relationships are fairly strong.

In the former table, we can see that home ownership does seem to make a difference. Home owners are more likely than renters to generally oppose facility siting and to oppose it in their respective cities or towns. Renters are somewhat more likely to favor siting treatment facilities locally and are less likely to be NIMBY Syndromers.

When we look at length of residence, longer-term residents resemble home owners in their attitudinal profiles. For ease of illustration, Table 4.7 presents length of residence in two categories—one for people who reported living in the city or town for fewer than five years and another for people who said they lived in the community for five years or more. Longer term residents are less likely than shorter term residents to favor treatment facilities anywhere in the state, and are more likely to oppose facilities anywhere in the state. Longer term residents are also more likely to be NIMBY Syndromers.

THE POLITICAL DIMENSION: PARTISAN AND POLITICAL ACTIVITY CORRELATES OF OPPOSITION

Perhaps the greatest concerns associated with opposition attitudes flows from an expected relationship with different types of political activity and partisanship. One of the fears expressed by

Table 4.6
**The Relationship Between Home Ownership and Opposition to Treatment
Facility Siting in Five Massachusetts Cities and Towns Combined**

| | Housing Status | |
	Own Home	Rent
Favor or mostly favor siting in state and local community	30.3%	38.9%
Oppose or mostly oppose siting in both state and local community	43.0%	39.7%
NIMBY - Favor or mostly favor in state but not in local community	26.7%	21.4%
Total percent	100.0%	100.0%
n	972	519

Pearson Chi-square = 12.11   Significance = .00

parties wishing to site treatment facilities is the idea that the
people who most oppose facility siting are people who are highly
politically active. The worry is that once opposition to a proposed
facility materializes, local organizations quickly form to politically oppose the facility. Yet we have very little information about
whether people who tend to oppose facilities are indeed people
who tend to be more politically active or more politically partisan
in general. A relationship has been found between partisan
identification and concern about the environment (Buttel and
Flinn, 1978a). We don't know empirically whether such patterns
extend to the specific instance of siting hazardous waste facilities.
We present these relationships in Tables 4.8 and 4.9 and find some
surprising results.

We looked at the issue of political activity by asking respondents two questions about their previous experience in specific
activities. We looked at whether the respondent had ever taken

Table 4.7
The Relationship Between Length of Residence and Attitudes Toward Facility Siting in Five Massachusetts Cities and Towns Combined

| | Length of residence in city or town | |
	Fewer than five years	Five years or more
Favor or mostly favor siting in state and local community	41.3%	31.3%
Oppose or mostly oppose siting in both state and local community	38.0%	42.7%
NIMBY - Favor or mostly favor in state but not in local community	20.7%	26.0%
Total percent	100.0%	100.0%
n	305	1199

Pearson Chi-square = 11.42   Significance = .00

part in a local political campaign and whether the respondent had ever attended an anti-nuclear rally. While we would not expect large numbers of people to report having participated in the latter, answers might be indicative of a group of people more likely to act on an ideologically grounded form of political behavior, and may reveal a core group of people with significantly different attitudes toward facility siting.

These results, shown in Table 4.8, indicate that prior political activity experience has little relation to attitudes toward siting. Indeed, people with prior campaign experience are not more likely than non-participants to oppose or favor siting in any way. This is also true for people who reported having taken part in anti-nuclear rallies. People who are opposed to facility siting do not seem to differ in the extent to which they are politically experienced. We, of course, cannot tell whether opposers who

Table 4.8
The Relationship Between Political Activity and Attitudes Toward Hazardous Waste Treatment Facility Siting in Five Massachusetts Cities and Towns Combined

	Type of Prior Political Activity				
	Has respondent ever taken part in a political campaign?			Has respondent ever taken part in an anti-nuclear rally?	
	Yes	No		Yes	No
Favor or mostly favor siting in state and local community	33.8%	33.3%		26.3%	34.0%
Oppose or mostly oppose siting in both state and local community	39.7%	42.3%		47.4%	41.2%
NIMBY - Favor or mostly favor in state but not in local community	26.5%	24.4%		26.3%	24.8%
Total percent	100.0%	100.0%		100.0%	100.0%
n	390	1126		114	1402
	Pearson Chi-square = 0.93			Pearson Chi-square = 2.94	
	Significance = .63			Significance = .23	

have been politically active in the past are more likely to be politically active in their opposition to facility siting.

When we look at the partisan nature of the respondents, we develop this picture a little more clearly. In Table 4.9 we correlated the respondents' partisan identifications, that is, whether they consider themselves to be Republicans, independents (having no party identification), or Democrats. These results show some interesting patterns. All three party identification groups of people tend to equally favor or mostly favor facility siting. However, independents and Democrats are very similar in their propensities to generally oppose facility siting anywhere in the state. Well over forty percent of each of these groups of people

Table 4.9
The Relationship Between Party Identification and Attitudes Toward Treatment Facility Siting in Five Massachusetts Cities and Towns Combined

	Party Identification		
	Republican	Independent (none)	Democrat
Favor or mostly favor siting in state and local community	35.1%	28.7%	33.3%
Oppose or mostly oppose siting in both state and local community	33.9%	46.2%	43.4%
NIMBY – Favor or mostly favor in state but not in local community	31.0%	25.1%	23.3%
Total percent	100.0%	100.0%	100.0%
n	316	251	896

Pearson Chi-square = 13.81   Significance = .00

oppose or mostly oppose siting a facility anywhere in the state. Republicans, on the other hand, are less likely than either independents or Democrats to oppose siting anywhere in the state, but are more likely to be NIMBY Syndromers. Republicans tend more than either of the other two partisan groups to be in favor of facility siting as long as it is not in their backyards.

OPPOSITION AND THE ROLE OF THE MEDIA

One of the emerging factors identified as a major influence on the level of opposition to facility siting is the role of the media, especially the local print medium. In particular, Mazur (1989) has argued that media coverage of proposals to site facilities is largely responsible for the shape of public opposition. Mazur's thesis suggests that it matters little whether the media are positive or negative toward a particular siting effort. In his view, the more media coverage there is, the more likely people will become opposed to facility siting. In his words:

> high news coverage of a waste site not only raises public concern, but pushes it toward opposition to the site, raising fears in the adjacent community, and generally working against the siting of waste disposal facilities. (119)

If Mazur's thesis has applicability to treatment facility siting, the level of media coverage should be correlated with the level of opposition. The data at hand, however, should provide us with a rather unique way of looking at this thesis. Our interviews were conducted with respondents who were not facing the imminent prospect of having a waste facility sited near them and, therefore, there could be no issue-specific media coverage. Rather, the siting was a purely hypothetical possibility. In this case, we can try to ascertain whether, as an extension of Mazur's argument, people who read more in the local media about hazardous waste issues are the people who most oppose facility siting.

To look at this, we asked respondents in our national survey to provide us with information about a range of media-related activities. We did not ask respondents specifically about frequency of exposure to news stories about hazardous waste or related issues. We simply asked about general practices of reading newspapers and watching the news on television. However, if media exposure helps to push people toward opposition, we would still expect people with the greatest media exposure to exhibit more opposition than people with little or no media exposure. This hypothesis is investigated in Tables 4.10 and 4.11.

In Table 4.10, which refers to reading newspapers, we see that most people tend to be generally opposed to facility siting except for those who read newspapers only several times a week. The tendency is for people who report reading newspapers several times a week to be disproportionately NIMBY Syndromers. Clearly, there is no linear trend suggesting that the more exposure

Table 4.10
The Relationship Between Newspaper Exposure and Opposition to Hazardous Waste Treatment Facilities in the National Sample

| | Reading Newspapers* | | | |
	Daily	Several times a week	Once a week	Less than once a week
Favor or mostly favor siting in state and local community	14.4%	14.7%	12.5%	28.0%
Oppose or mostly oppose siting in both state and local community	64.4%	19.3%	50.0%	57.0%
NIMBY - Favor or mostly favor in state but not in local community	21.2%	66.0%	37.5%	15.0%
Total percent	100.0%	100.0%	100.0%	100.0%
n	146	109	24	93

Pearson Chi-square = 85.64   Significance = .00

* *Question wording*: "About how often do you read a newspaper? Do you read a newspaper *every day, several times a week, about once a week,* or *less than once a week*?"

one has to newspapers the more likely one is to oppose facility siting or to exhibit the NIMBY Syndrome.

This is not necessarily the case with watching television news. The general pattern revealed in Table 4.11 is that people at all levels of exposure to television news tend to be NIMBY Syndromers except those who watch television news daily. Daily TV news viewers tend to be disproportionately generally opposed. Although there are many reasons to discount these results, not the least of which is that the questions we asked were not directed specifically to exposure to environmentally relevant information through the media, there does not seem to be much support here for the media exposure hypothesis.

Table 4.11
The Relationship Between Television News Exposure and Opposition to Hazardous Waste Treatment Facilities in the National Sample

| | Watching News on TV* | | | |
	Daily	Several times a week	Once a week	Less than once a week
Favor or mostly favor siting in state and local community	19.9%	16.5%	16.7%	19.4%
Oppose or mostly oppose siting in both state and local community	54.1%	21.1%	33.3%	33.3%
NIMBY – Favor or mostly favor in state but not in local community	26.0%	62.4%	50.0%	47.3%
Total percent	100.0%	100.0%	100.0%	100.0%
n	146	109	24	93

Pearson Chi-square = 59.5   Significance = .00

* *Question wording*: "About how many nights a week do you watch the news on television, either network or local? Do you watch the news *every day*, *several times a week*, *about once a week*, or *less than once a week*?"

THE RISK-PERCEPTION ROOTS OF OPPOSITION

Up until now, most of the variables we have analyzed constitute objective and/or demographic traits of the respondents. We have not examined much in the way of attitudinal antecedents to opposition. However, we would probably expect the way one perceives the prospective hazardous waste facility to play a paramount role in determining whether one is willing to accept or opposes the siting of such a facility (Berman and Wandersman, 1990; USEPA, 1979; Portney, 1986). Indeed, we can even conceptualize this variable as intervening in the relationships between the demographic characteristics and opposition. In this way, the demographic characteristics might be said to influence whether respondents perceive a proposed facility constitutes a major health threat. Once people perceive a facility as a potential health threat, opposition almost naturally follows.

In order to look at how people perceive the facility, we asked respondents some direct questions. After we asked people about their attitudes toward siting a facility in the state, then in their respective communities, we asked them to tell us the reasons why they felt the way they did. In particular, we prompted them to tell us what kinds of events or scenarios they associated with a facility if it were actually built in their communities. We recorded these responses in their actual "raw" form. Upon examination of the actual responses, we can assess each one to determine whether it seems to contain any sense of health threat implied or imposed by the hypothetical presence of the facility. The answers we considered to be reflective of health threat risk perception are summarized in Table 4.12. In general, when people said they thought of the facility being too dangerous, that they feared contamination of groundwater, and so on, we categorized these responses as being "health threat" responses. Some people responded with non-health threat perceptions, such as "property taxes will go up," "property values will go down," "it wouldn't help the city's image," and so on.

With the simple distinction between health risk and non-health risk perceptions, we can see if there is a correlation with the types of opposition to facility siting. These results are presented in Table 4.13. Here it is very clear that perception of an impending health threat is an extremely strong correlate of opposition, far stronger than any of the correlates we investigated so far. People citing non-health threat fears are much more likely to favor or mostly favor a facility than people citing health threat issues. The health threat perception seems most closely associated with general opposition to locating a facility anywhere in the state. But it is also associated with the NIMBY Syndrome. People who fear the health consequences of locating a facility in their community are somewhat more likely to be NIMBY Syndromers than people who fear economic and non-health consequences.

Table 4.12
Perceived Consequences of Having a Hazardous Waste Treatment Facility Sited in Respondents' Communities

			Sample:		
United States			Five Communities Combined		
Reason	Number n=400	Percent	Reason	Number n=1026	Percent
Health Risk Responses					
Unsafe, dangerous	126	33.0%	Unsafe	259	26.0%
Too close to to be safe	20	5.2%	Don't trust managers to keep it safe	73	7.3%
They don't know how to make it safe	36	9.4%	Risk of accident	64	6.4%
Not worth the risk	30	7.9%	Will pollute	20	2.0%
Risk of accident	32	8.4%	Too close to people to be safe	125	12.5%
Endanger food	8	2.1%	Inadequate technology to make safe	32	3.2%
Don't trust companies to make it safe	20	5.2%	Fear water pollution	60	6.0%
Storage dangers	6	1.6%	Local officials can't control safety	5	0.5%
Bad health consequences	6	1.6%	Safer to put it elsewhere	6	0.6%
Contaminate drinking water	2	0.5%	Not safe to put it anywhere in my town	6	0.6%
Not enough safety precautions	2	0.5%			
Pollute air	2	0.5%			
Non-Health Risk Responses					
Gives us someone else's waste	4	1.0%	No space/land	130	13.0%
Too few benefits	4	1.0%	Devalue property	9	0.9%
Causes disruption	8	2.1%	No more here	2	0.2%
Heard stories	2	0.5%	Just oppose	19	1.9%
No space/land	14	3.7%	Don't need it	29	2.9%
Already enough	8	2.1%	Make city dirty	12	1.2%
Devalue properties	4	1.0%	Already enough	25	2.5%
Don't have enough information	12	3.1%	Inequitable to put it here	48	4.8%
Looks awful	22	5.8%	Won't help city	4	0.4%
Too noisy	2	0.5%	Need specifics	25	2.5%
Attracts other industries	2	0.5%	Taxes would go up	1	0.1%
			Everyone opposes	11	1.1%
No reason given	10	2.7%	Its producers' responsibility	2	0.2%
			Hurts tourism	30	3.0%
			No reason given	29	2.9%

Table 4.13
The Relationship Between Health Risk Perception and Opposition to Siting a Hazardous Waste Treatment Facility in Respondents' Communities

	Did Respondent Give a Health Risk Response to the Hypothetical Facility Siting?			
	Massachusetts		Nationwide	
	No	Yes	No	Yes
Favor or mostly favor siting in state and local community	56.6%	0.3%	52.9%	8.0%
Oppose or mostly oppose siting in both state and local community	22.7%	68.5%	19.2%	56.5%
NIMBY - Favor or mostly favor in state but not in local community	20.7%	31.2%	27.9%	35.5%
Total percent	100.0%	100.0%	100.0%	100.0%
n	347	650	82	290
Pearson chi-square	564.2		388.0	
Significance	.0000		.0000	

SUMMARY OF THE CORRELATES OF OPPOSITION

While these cross-tabulations provide a description of simple correlations with opposition to treatment facility siting, they may not reflect "independent" influences. For example, it may well be that there is a close relationship between income and Republican party identification, or between home ownership and length of residence. It has been suggested that there is a relationship between gender and level of knowledge (Arcury, Scollay, and Johnson, 1987). In order to make an effort to sort out the independent influences of each variable, we can develop a simple multi-variate log-linear model. Initially, we would like to know the effects of each variable controlling for the others. This is precisely the type of task for which multi-variate analysis was designed. Here, because of the nominal and ordinal coding of the variables, we rely on log-linear analysis.

The results of these initial log-linear analyses are found in Table 4.14, where general opposition to siting anywhere in the state is the dependent variable in the top portion of the table, and opposition only to local siting, or the NIMBY Syndrome, is the dependent variable in the lower portion.[2] In these analyses, we focus on some ten independent variables available only in the five-city samples. Here we see that the pattern of relationships is generally consistent with those revealed in the cross-tabulations.

There are several notable patterns. First, only five variables seem to be strongly related to general opposition to siting anywhere in the state when the influences of other variables are controlled: by far, the perception of health risk is the strongest; female gender, having low income, and both interaction terms (i.e., women with children and women who perceive a health risk) are also important, albeit less strong, influences. Clearly, people who perceive the site to pose a health risk are much more likely to oppose siting the facility anywhere in the state. Women are more likely than men to oppose siting a facility anywhere in the state; women with children are more likely to oppose siting anywhere in the state than women with no children; and women who perceive a significant health threat are more likely than women who do not perceive a health threat to oppose siting in the state.

Second, a propensity to exhibit the NIMBY Syndrome is highly related to the perception of health risk, Republican party identification, level of knowledge, low income, and length of residence. The NIMBY Syndrome seems to be most prominent among people who believe a treatment facility poses a major health risk, people who think of themselves as Republicans, people who have the highest level of knowledge about hazardous waste, and people who have low incomes. Perhaps most interesting, controlling for these factors, people who have lived in their communities for

Table 4.14
Multiple Log-Linear Results Showing the Influences on Opposition to Hazardous Waste Facility Siting in Five Massachusetts Cities and Towns

Dependent Variable: Opposition to Siting Anywhere in the State

Independent Variables	Coefficient	Z-score
Perception of health risk	.521	16.57**
Female gender	.132	4.17**
Party (Republican)	-.009	-0.25
Low income	.068	1.99*
Homeownership	-.011	-0.31
Level of knowledge	.014	0.41
Length of residence	-.015	-0.40
Children in house	.049	1.52
Female-children interaction	.066	2.08*
Female-risk interaction	.061	1.97*

L^2 = 206.2   D.F. = 177   Probability = .005

Dependent Variable: NIMBY Syndrome - Opposition to Siting in Local Community

Independent Variables	Coefficient	Z-score
Perception of health risk	.169	5.64**
Female gender	-.013	-0.44
Party (Republican)	.242	7.63**
Low income	.100	3.00**
Homeownership	.003	0.04
Level of knowledge	.241	7.58**
Length of residence	-.088	-2.55*
Children in house	-.016	0.50
Female-children interaction	-.006	-0.21
Female-risk interaction	.086	2.86**

L^2 = 289.2   D.F. = 177   Probability = .000

  * Significant at .05 level
** Significant at .01 level or beyond

more than five years actually are less likely to exhibit the NIMBY Syndrome.

PUBLIC OPPOSITION: A SELF-REINFORCING AND DEGENERATIVE PROCESS

If the opposition to treatment facility siting is as strong and as unyielding as these data imply, then there must be something more fundamental and powerful acting as determinants than the influences we have been able to investigate here. Indeed, we have already alluded to some of those dynamic influences earlier. But we can reconsider the range of these influences in light of the results of our empirical investigation. As we suggested earlier, the data we have analyzed do not complete the picture of public opposition. Nevertheless, the results are consistent with a dynamic process which determines how people will eventually respond if faced with the prospect of having a treatment facility sited in their communities.

The strength of the relationship between a fear of a health risk and safety consequences is consistent with a contingent interpretation of the siting process. Initially, there is a strong tendency for people to be inclined to oppose facility siting in their communities. Many people, especially women, tend to be predisposed to oppose siting treatment facilities anywhere. If a proposal is actually put forth to site such a facility, a process begins which almost seems to guarantee that opposition will increase. Many people receive information about the siting proposal through a screen of concern about public health and safety. Perhaps they are looking for additional information to allay their fears, to alter the screen through which the initial proposal is viewed, but no such information emerges. Instead, nearly every subsequent event reinforces people's views that the proposed facility will be unsafe. People with higher incomes, who have lived in the community longer, and who are Republicans tend to be especially sensitive to appeals calling for diminished opposition. The result is that many people develop an entrenched opposition to local siting. Thus, the initial opposition or inclination to oppose is simply strengthened by subsequent events.

WHAT INFLUENCES PUBLIC OPPOSITION: A SUMMARY

Our initial investigation in this chapter focused on the correlates of attitudinal opposition to treatment facility siting. The way we looked at opposition allowed us to build a picture of who favors and who generally opposes facility siting, and who tends to exhibit the NIMBY Syndrome. The results showed that those generally opposed tend to be low income people, and women, especially women with children and women who perceive treatment facilities as posing health threats. People who exhibit the NIMBY Syndrome, favoring a facility somewhere in the state but not in their communities, tend to be low income people; people with the very highest levels of environmental knowledge and information; people who have lived in their respective communities for less than five years; people who identify themselves as Republicans; and people who perceive the facility as posing a major health threat, especially women who perceive a health threat.

Despite these patterns, risk perception seems to be a consistently stronger influence on opposition than any of the demographic characteristics. Clearly, people who associate health risk events or health problems with a treatment facility are considerably more likely than people who associate non-health risk consequences to oppose siting a facility. Fear of health consequences constitutes the single most important influence on opposition among those influences we were able to investigate.

All of this points to several major conclusions. First, attitudes in opposition to local facility siting are very strong. Second, opposition to local siting is quite strongly influenced by a perception of the dangers or risks associated, whether correctly or incorrectly, with hazardous waste treatment facilities. Third, if opposition is to be diminished, ways have to be found to affect people's perceptions that treatment facilities are dangerous. Whether there is anything that can affect these perceptions is not obvious from the analysis in this chapter. As we have argued earlier, the establishment of correlations may not tell us anything about attitude change. It is to this issue, the correlates of changes in people's opposition and perceptions of health threat, that we turn our attention in Chapter 5.

NOTES

1. The income categories are as follows: Low income—between $0 and $15,000 in 1983 income from all sources in household; Middle income—between $15,001 and $30,000; and High income—over $30,001. People who responded that they were on welfare and did not give an amount were included in the low income category. People who refused to answer were excluded from this analysis.

2. All independent variables have dichotomous (0–1) coding. The low income category reflects whether or not the respondent was in the lowest income category reported in Table 4.1. Level of knowledge reflects whether or not the respondent answered all five questions correctly. Each dependent variable is coded as a dichotomous (0–1) variable.

Chapter 5

Correlates of Changes in Public Opposition: What Changes Minds

Since public opposition to hazardous waste treatment facilities appears to be so widespread, it becomes important not only to understand the correlates of that opposition (as we sought to do in Chapter 4), but also to understand what, if anything, seems to be correlated with change in that opposition. If there is any validity to the argument we made in Chapter 2 concerning prescriptions derived from casually observed correlations with opposition, then even the more systematically observed correlates of opposition may well provide us with no useful information about what can be done to *change* the level of opposition. Based on the correlations reported in Chapter 4, we might be tempted, for example, to infer that if people's perceptions of risk associated with a treatment facility could somehow be changed, then their opposition would also change. Yet this is an inference that may not be warranted from the results we have presented so far.

It is true that people who perceive the health risks to be high are among the people most opposed to siting facilities either in the state or locally. But this does not necessarily mean that changing people's perceptions of health risk will change their opposition. In order to develop specific information on this point, we need to examine characteristics of attitudinal change. Using survey research results, however, we can make a preliminary effort to examine what seem to be the most salient reasons why people change their attitudes away from overt opposition to at least passive acceptance. This is a slightly different empirical research problem than examining the correlates of opposition itself.

THE DEFINITION OF ATTITUDE CHANGE

In order to examine attitudinal change, it is customary and most appropriate to rely on information derived from panel design surveys where the same individuals are re-interviewed at at least two different points in time. Unfortunately, this type of data is not available. Consequently, we rely on another method for assessing attitudinal change. In this case, we identify respondents who seem to exhibit a propensity to change their minds based on an apparent willingness to conditionally accept a facility rather than people who can be said to have actually changed their minds. To do this, we rely on answers respondents gave us to the hypothetical questions analyzed in Chapter 2. Based on the answers to these questions, we essentially divide respondents into three groups of people: people who favor or mostly favor facility siting in their respective communities (we assume that these people's attitudes would not have to change since they already find siting acceptable); people who initially opposed the facility but who changed their minds in response to at least one of the eleven compensation or risk mitigation proposals; and people who initially opposed facility siting and did not change their minds in response to any proposal.

The focus of this analysis will be on those people who changed in response to at least one proposal compared to the other two groups. Quite obviously, these data cannot be interpreted to reflect increases or decreases in opposition; they simply give us some insight into whether individuals who initially oppose facility siting seem to be susceptible to changing their opposition, and whether these people seem to differ in important ways from their non-changing counterparts who initially opposed siting.

The independent variables we investigate as correlates of change in opposition parallel those presented in Chapter 4. We provide the basic cross-tabulations of income, level of knowledge, gender, home ownership, length of residence, political party identification, and perception of health risk with change in opposition in Tables 5.1 through 5.7. Table 5.8 presents the multiple log-linear analysis to help us assess the independent effects of each possible explanation. These tables are based only on respondents who initially opposed local facility siting.

The reason why we focus on the same independent variables as found in Chapter 4 are twofold. First, given the definition of attitude change (the propensity to change), we have no measures of change in the independent variables. In other words, we have no independent measures of changes in variables such as the perception of health risk, length of residence, and income. If our analysis were based on data from a panel survey where the same people were reinterviewed at multiple time points, we could attempt to track changes in attitudes and correlate these changes with changes in other characteristics. Unfortunately, because we do not rely on panel data, our independent variables cannot measure changes. Second, there is not very much theory to suggest that the correlates of change should be expected to be any different than the correlates of opposition in the first place. Whether this can be said to be empirically accurate is a question which could perhaps be entertained after examination of the results in this chapter.

THE CORRELATES OF CHANGE IN OPPOSITION

Table 5.1 reveals that there is a modest tendency for lower-income people to be willing to change their minds and to accept a facility. This is to be expected given our definition of attitude change. Clearly, the compensation proposals which served as the stimulus for change seem more likely to appeal to people who are less well-off economically. A person struggling to make ends meet is probably more likely to find a promise of increased job opportunity appealing than someone who is financially better off.

Table 5.1
The Relationship Between Family Income and Change in Opposition to Local Facility Siting Among Initial Opposers

	Family Income		
	Low	Middle	High
Changed to favor or mostly favor local siting	41.4%	30.9%	26.4%
Still opposed to local siting	58.6%	69.1%	73.6%
Totals	100.0%	100.0%	100.0%
n	273	320	276

Pearson Chi-square = 14.7   Significance = .00

The level of knowledge respondents have about hazardous waste, the respondent's gender, length of residence, and political party identification are essentially unrelated to a propensity to change one's mind about facility siting. There is only a very slight tendency for people with the least knowledge to maintain their opposition. Men and women drop their opposition about equally, which is somewhat consistent with other research on gender differences in attitude change toward siting nuclear facilities after the Three-Mile Island accident (Nealy, Melber, and Rankin, 1983). People who lived in their respective communities fewer than five years show only a slight tendency to change their minds. And people who identify themselves as Republicans, Democrats, or independents are all about equally likely to drop their opposition.

On the other hand, home ownership does seem to make something of a difference. As shown in Table 5.6, homeowners are considerably less likely than renters to change their minds. This is true despite the fact that renters were somewhat more accepting of the facility proposal in the first place. Owning one's own home apparently gives people sufficient tangible stake in a

Table 5.2

The Relationship Between Level of Knowledge About Hazardous Waste and Change in Opposition to Local Siting Among Initial Opposers

	Number of Hazardous Substances Correctly Identified					
	0	1	2	3	4	5
Changed to favor or mostly favor local siting	20.0%	33.3%	31.0%	32.7%	31.9%	29.5%
Still opposed to local siting	80.0%	66.7%	69.0%	67.3%	68.1%	70.5%
Total	100.0%	100.0%	100.0%	100.0%	100.0%	100.0%
n	10	42	129	248	379	227

Pearson Chi-square = 1.29   Significance = .93

Table 5.3

The Relationship Between Gender and Change in Opposition to Local Facility Siting Among Initial Opposers

	Gender	
	Male	Female
Changed to favor or mostly favor local siting	30.2%	32.2%
Still opposed to local siting	69.8%	67.8%
Totals	100.0%	100.0%
n	427	608

Pearson Chi-square = 0.48   Significance = .49

Table 5.4
The Relationship Between Length of Residence and Change in Opposition to Local Facility Siting Among Initial Opposers

	Length of Residence in city or town	
	Fewer than five years	Five years or more
Changed to favor or mostly favor local siting	36.3%	31.1%
Still opposed to local siting	63.7%	68.9%
Totals	100.0%	100.0%
n	179	824

Pearson Chi-square = 1.86   Significance = .17

Table 5.5
The Relationship Between Political Party Identification and Change in Opposition to Local Siting Among Initial Opposers

	Political Party Identification		
	Republican	Independent	Democrat
Changed to favor or mostly favor local siting	34.6%	30.7%	31.1%
Still opposed to local siting	65.4%	69.3%	68.9%
Totals	100.0%	100.0%	100.0%
n	205	179	598

Pearson Chi-square = 0.99   Significance = .61

Table 5.6
The Relationship Between Home Ownership and Change in Opposition to Local Siting Among Initial Opposers

	Housing Status	
	Renters	Homeowners
Changed to favor or mostly favor local siting	38.2%	29.2%
Still opposed to local siting	61.8%	70.8%
Totals	100.0%	100.0%
n	317	677

Pearson Chi-square = 7.88   Significance = .00

community to make them unwilling to accept a treatment facility even in the face of the economic compensation and risk mitigation proposals. This might be due to the fact that homeowners tend to have higher incomes than renters, and we will later attempt to sort out the independent influences of these variables.

Finally, the perception of health risk is closely related to change. Consistent with the earlier patterns, people who fear health consequences of having a facility built in their communities are much less likely than people who fear non-health consequences to be willing to change their minds. As presented in Table 5.7, most of the people in both groups do not change their minds, but people who worry about non-health effects are about fifty percent more likely than their health risk counterparts to change their minds.

As we did when we analyzed types of opposition, we can attempt to sort out the independent effects of these variables using multi-variate log-linear analysis. Table 5.8 presents this analyses. By looking at the direction or the sign of the relationships we can make inferences about which groups tend to be more or less likely to change their minds about opposing the facility. Since the

Table 5.7
The Relationship Between Perception of Health Risk and Change in Opposition to Local Siting Among Initial Opposers

	Did Respondent Give a Health Risk Response to the Hypothetical Facility Siting?	
	No	Yes
Changed to favor or mostly favor local siting	37.0%	28.0%
Still opposed to local siting	63.0%	72.0%
Totals	100.0%	100.0%
n	392	643

Pearson Chi-square = 9.14   Significance = .00

dependent variable is a measure of whether people seemed to be willing to change or drop their opposition to local siting, independent variables with a positive sign reflect variables which are associated with change in attitude, that is, changing from opposition to non-opposition of the facility. On the other hand, variables carrying a negative sign are those which are associated with non-change of attitudes toward the facility, such as continuing to oppose the facility.

Here we can see that among the variables in the model, when the effects of the other variables are controlled, four variables seem to reduce opposition and two increase opposition. People with lower incomes are more likely to change their minds (suggesting that people with higher incomes are less likely to change their minds); Republicans, people with high levels of knowledge, and women who perceive a high health risk are more likely to be willing to change their minds. People who perceive a serious health threat and people who have lived in the community for more than five years are less likely to change their minds.

These results still do not provide us with major insights useful in understanding changes in attitudes toward local siting of

Table 5.8
Multiple Log-Linear Results Showing the Influences on Change in Opposition to Local Facility Siting

Dependent Variable: Change in Opposition to Local Siting		
Independent Variables	Coefficient	Z-score
Perception of health risk	-.192	-6.16**
Female gender	.052	1.66
Party (Republican)	.221	6.73**
Low income	.246	7.25**
Homeownership	-.057	-1.62
Level of knowledge	.165	4.99**
Length of residence	-.142	-4.07**
Children in house	.072	2.25*
Female-children interaction	.041	1.31
Female-risk interaction	.093	2.99*
L^2 = 324.6	D.F. = 177	Probability = .000

 * Significant at .05 level
** Significant at .01 level or beyond

treatment facilities. It does suggest that attitude change, to the extent that it can be inferred from the measures used here, is not produced in any patterned way, at least not in any way that would seem to lend itself to public interventions. It does seem clear that health risk perception could be a major influence either directly or indirectly on attitudes toward prospective facilities. The next logical question, therefore, is: what, if anything, changes people's perceptions of the health risks associated with treatment facility siting. Unfortunately, the projects reported here have no direct way of measuring whether or the extent to which health risk perception changes. Therefore, it is not possible for us to examine this question empirically.

There is some existing analysis which bears on the question of what causes people's health risk perceptions to increase—what makes people perceive that a facility poses a greater risk then they previously thought. For example, Mazur's (1989) analysis argues that media exposure plays a dominant role. In this analysis, the argument is that people perceive the facility to be increasingly dangerous as they are exposed to more and more media reports of a facility. As we noted before, Mazur's analysis suggests that it does not matter whether the media coverage is positive or negative toward the prospective facility, it will have the effect of increasing people's opposition by increasing their perceptions of health risk. After people perceive the risks to be quite high, their perceptions of health risks can subsequently be reduced with the absence of media exposure. Thus, according to the logic of this analysis, the way to diminish people's perceptions of health risk is to make sure they hear nothing about the facility through the media. Media exposure, however, is most certainly something that cannot be controlled as a matter of public policy. Thus, if attitude change is required for successful siting, then it will have to look elsewhere.

All of this points to the desperate need to develop better information and to conduct explicit research on changes in risk perceptions over time. Until more research is available, it is unlikely that we will be able to develop a clearer picture of what, if anything, can be done to reduce people's risk perceptions associated with hazardous waste treatment facilities. Until such research results are available, it does not seem very likely that public policy will be able to prescribe processes capable of leading to successful siting.

THE CORRELATES OF CHANGE IN OPPOSITION

A Summary and Implications

What can we infer from these results? Consistent with previous results reported here, it seems quite clear that wealthier people, people who have lived in the respective communities for more than five years, and people who perceive that a hazardous waste facility carries substantial health risks are the people least likely to be accepting of compensation and mitigation proposals. Their attitudes are the least likely to change. Does this mean that nothing can be done to change people's minds about facility siting? Obviously such a conclusion would exceed the power of the data we have been able to generate here. We can say, however, that there is little evidence that any one type of person seems more prone to be influenced by compensation and risk mitigation efforts. It is also clear that better sources of data, preferably information about actual attitude change in response to specific siting efforts, are needed to expand our base of knowledge about who changes their minds and why.

Our subsequent analysis focused on the characteristics of people who changed their minds to drop their opposition in response to the eleven compensation and risk mitigation proposals we investigated in Chapter 2. Here we found that people who changed their minds tended to be poorer, more Republican, more knowledgeable about hazardous waste, and more likely to be women who perceive a health risk from the facility, compared to people who did not change their minds. It seems clear from these results that indeed, people who perceive a relatively high level of health risk from a hazardous waste treatment facility and people who have lived longer in their respective communities seem to be the least likely to change their minds concerning local siting of facilities.

These results reveal good news and bad news for people advocating siting of treatment facilities. The good news is that there are some identifiable groups of people who seem to be more likely than others to be willing to change their minds and accept a facility. The bad news is that these people are not very numerous. As we noted earlier, the vast majority of people tend to perceive that the prospect of having a treatment facility nearby poses a significant health threat to them and/or their families. It is these people who appear to be among the least likely to change their minds—the least likely to drop their opposition.

Clearly there is a need for more robust and directed research on the subject of changes in risk perceptions, especially as applied to facility siting. Given the lack of clear evidence on what causes reductions in risk perceptions, there does not seem to be any particular reason to believe that public policy can effectively intervene to change people's attitudes and perceptions, especially those attitudes and perceptions associated with the health threat posed by a facility. If these conclusions represent accurate assessments of the context in which siting decisions are to be made, then hazardous waste management policy and its implementation must find a way to incorporate rather than try to change people's perceptions into their efforts. Before we conclude that these observations are accurate reflections of this context, we must investigate whether they seem to be grounded in more general theories of environmental and technological risks. This we do in Chapter 6.

Chapter 6

The Social, Cultural, and Psychological Construction of Opposition to Facility Siting: The Normative Bases of Conflict

Much of the conflict and disagreement over whether, how, and where to site hazardous waste treatment facilities takes place as part of a larger, more general set of disagreements which pervade our society. Many of the same fundamental arguments which emerge in any statewide or local attempt to implement facility siting as part of its hazardous waste management policy are present in nearly every aspect of environmental issues, decisions, and public policy making. In order to understand the true problems that treatment facility siting confronts, one must understand the normative context that underlies such decisions. We refer to the normative context as the "social, cultural, and psychological construction of opposition."

Our purpose in examining the social, cultural, and psychological construction of opposition is not to present a comprehensive picture of different views toward the role of culture and values in American social conflict. This would be much too formidable a task to attempt here. Rather, the purpose is to provide a picture of the background or context in which hazardous waste siting decisions are made. We are less interested here in whether conflict analysis is or should be pursued as a form of rational analysis, or whether such analysis is inevitably culture-bound. This idea has been discussed extensively elsewhere, especially with respect to the role that values play in our societal definitions and acceptance of different levels of risk (Douglas, 1985; Rayner,

1984; Douglas and Wildavsky, 1982a; Douglas and Wildavsky, 1982b; Thompson and Wildavsky, 1982; Rayner and Cantor, 1987; Berger and Luckman, 1967). Rather, our purpose here is to examine some of the major ways in which differences of opinion and differences in values seem to inform the decision-making processes associated with, and ultimately in opposition to, facility siting.

Paralleling the ideas found in the literature on the cultural construction of risk, when we speak of a "social, cultural, and psychological construction of opposition" to facility siting, we are suggesting that people's opposition to facility siting is rooted not in some absolute nature of danger from such a facility. Rather, it is rooted in a relative sense or perception of the dangers, a perception which is constructed and thereby recognized by people in a community. We can see the basis for these perceptions through an investigation into the value conflicts surrounding different types of environmental issues.

A number of normative disagreements have become rather explicit in efforts to resolve environmental problems over the past twenty years or so. These normative disagreements, in a sense, reveal recurring value conflicts which are deeply rooted in the American culture. One such normative disagreement pits reverence of the role of science and technology in solving problems against skepticism of science and technology's ability to do more than create new problems in pursuit of solutions to old problems. Another such normative disagreement involves values about the relationship between nature and society, or between the physical world and the people who inhabit it. A third normative disagreement involves the relationship between government and society, or the extent to which government is valued as an instrument of society. And a fourth disagreement involves distributional fairness, that is, who bears how much burden in order to produce social benefits. Each of these fundamental conflicts in values helps to form the basis of conflict over environmental issues, and treatment facility siting is no exception. In a sense, we might argue that these conflicts form the basic underpinnings of the NIMBY Syndrome.

THE SOCIAL AND CULTURAL CONSTRUCTION OF OPPOSITION

The Relationship Between Technology and Society

One of the most prominent normative underpinnings of treatment facility siting disagreements can be traced to different perceptions of the proper relationship between technology and society. Should science and technology be the driving force behind social innovation? Or should society, treating issues through a more humanistic approach, dictate the bounds of what science and technology attempt to do? Stated even more simply, should scientists have a free rein to determine the directions of society, or should society use science only for those purposes which are deemed desirable in their own right? This is a question that has persisted in many different contexts for generations.

There have been numerous exposés of the clash of these two perspectives, but none has expressed this type of value duality more clearly than that found in the works of the novelist C. P. Snow (1960; 1964). Snow describes the fundamental difficulties inherent in mutual understanding between what he calls "scientists" and "humanists." To Snow, difficulties in reaching such a mutual understanding flow from the fact that these groups speak very different languages. Scientists are acculturated into a set of beliefs and normative prescriptions about the role of science in society, about the proper way to conduct scientific inquiry, and about the value of the results of scientific inquiry to society. Humanists, on the other hand, tend to reject many of the beliefs and normative underpinnings of science, instead preferring to emphasize the need to humanize, subjectify, and contextualize each decision under consideration. Humanists tend to see science not as providing final answers to social problems but rather as displacing problems—that is, creating new problems but shifting them to someone else, someplace else, or sometime in the future (Dryzek, 1987).

Each of these cultures approaches being what one might call a "paradigm." A paradigm is simply a widely held set of beliefs about a particular or general subject. A paradigm is commonly said to exist when there is a high level of agreement with its tenets. For example, for many years, Einstein's theory of relativity was said to be the dominant paradigm in physics. It has been suggested that "scientism" and "humanism" also constitute something akin to paradigms, at least for the people who practice them. In elaborating the ways that this clash of cultures as paradigms affects environmental decisions, Cotgrove explains:

> It is because protagonists to the debate approach issues from different culture contexts, which generate different and conflicting implicit meanings, that there is mutual exasperation and charges and countercharges of irrationality and unreason. What is sensible from one point of view is nonsense from another. It is the implicit, self-evident, taken-for-granted character of paradigms which clogs the channels of communication. (1982:82)

This clash of cultures has clear and important implications for the definition and acceptance of different kinds of risks in society. The scientific approach to risks relies on given standards and methodologies applied in an "objective" fashion. The idea is that the amount and type of risk posed can be estimated through rigorous quantification and measurement, and adherence to the scientific method. Thus, the scientific approaches to risk lend themselves to the development of unique, detailed, and very technical language and concepts that one might suggest comes close to constituting a culture (Dietz and Rycroft, 1987). The scientific approach to risks purposely avoids discussion of value positions until the amount and type of risk are objectively estimated. Once estimated, the risk can be evaluated subjectively to decide whether it is worthwhile or should be avoided or changed through purposeful actions (Wilson and Crouch, 1987; Morone and Woodhouse, 1986). Indeed, Kraft and Vig (1988) suggest that this constitutes something of an instrumental view of science and technology where technology is thought of as being value neutral. According to this view, it is the purposes and uses of technology as decided by humans which determines whether it is something to be positively or negatively valued.

To the humanist, the estimation of risk cannot be accomplished in such a neat and value-free way. The humanist tends to see the scientific approach and associated methodologies as being rather limited forms of human expression. The humanist tends to feel the need to consider the broader range of human concerns about a given risk from the outset. To the humanist, the scientist's value-neutral analysis is a myth—instead of being value free, scientific methodologies carry with them implicit values at all levels (Wynne, 1982).

Although it may be something of an oversimplification to aggregate those alternative views under the rubric "humanism," it does capture at least one element of an important distinction reflected in local siting decisions. The risk implications of the clash of cultures as reflected in hazardous waste facility siting decisions are quite clear. For many people, decisions to site facilities constitute clashes between "experts," who want to site a facility in a specific location based on objective analysis, and the "public," which does not want it there. The public tends to take on decidedly humanist roles, often arguing that the experts could not have conducted value-free assessments of the risks and other characteristics of the particular site. Consequently, the public tends to distrust the experts and to believe that experts' conclusions are seriously flawed. We can see some basic reflections of this in the data we discussed in relation to "trust" in Chapter 3. Although we did not ask explicitly about the extent of trust people have in experts, respondents were able to volunteer such a feeling if they so desired. As Table 3.1 shows, only about 3.6 percent of the respondents suggested that they "most trusted" experts. More than twice as many people volunteered that they trusted no one.

The experts, on the other hand, often perceive that they are conducting the best possible analysis of the risks and costs associated with the specific site. In their minds, the public is totally irrational in its opposition to the facility. Their feeling is that if only the public could be made to understand the rational way the experts made their determination, then opposition would subside. Indeed, it has been suggested that this is the assumption which underlies current emphasis on "risk communication." To these people, risk communication means simply finding ways to explain to people why the experts are correct in their analyses and why the public is incorrect (Plough and Krimsky, 1987). The point is that because of the strict adherence by one or both parties in such conflicts to the idea that they are correct and the other is incorrect, both parties end up unable to communicate and subsequently resolve their differences. It is difficult to imagine how the types of tried siting methodologies described in Chapters 1 and 2 would be capable of overcoming such fundamental clashes of cultures.

The Relationship Between Nature and Society

Perhaps an even more deeply rooted clash of values can be found in the prescribed relationship between nature and society, or between the physical environment and the people who inhabit that environment. The type of relationship between nature and society carries with it inevitable links to economic issues. The issue is one of whether society's principle role, even obligation, is to conserve and protect the environment, or rather to economically exploit the environment for the benefit of humankind. There are clear traditions in American culture to support both positions (Buttel and Flinn, 1976).

Both positions can be traced to spiritual components of the Judeo-Christian tradition in America. In each position, the tradition starts with the belief in human dominion over the earth and its other living creatures. But this is about as far as the common tradition goes. The positions diverge in their interpretations of what "dominion" actually means. To the environmental conservationist, the value compares to St. Francis of Assisi's notion of human stewardship and protection of all God's creatures. To people such as Lynn White, this means that nature should be valued for its own sake and, therefore, people have a duty to protect nature from assaults resulting from economic market exploitation (White, 1967). To Ophuls (1977), the issue is one of protecting the environment for survival of humankind.

To today's advocates of free markets in the economy, the idea of dominion engenders a very different, perhaps even opposite, meaning. To these people, the idea of dominion is taken to mean that nature and its environment should be used in the service of society, directly toward the goal of bettering God's earthly kingdom. Consequently, these people often feel that they have an obligation to use the earth's resources and to economically exploit them for the betterment of humankind. Thus, these diametrically opposed definitions of dominion set the normative stage for specific clashes over environmental decisions.

As it applies to environmental issues, Lester Milbrath argues that the advocates of free-market approaches and proponents of the use of nature in the service of humankind are adherents to the "dominant social paradigm" (Milbrath, 1984). As such, he refers to these people as the environmental "rearguard" because they are defenders of this dominant social paradigm. On the other hand, he suggests that people who challenge this dominant social paradigm constitute the environmental "vanguard." Perhaps most importantly, Milbrath presents empirical information from a three-nation study (the United States, Great Britain, and West Germany) to support the idea that, indeed, there are these two distinctly different groups. Not everyone fits into these two groups, and the vast majority of people probably adhere to tenets of both. Implicit in Milbrath's argument, however, is the notion that social change toward adopting more of the vanguard's values will be necessary for the survival of the planet.

The manifestation of this set of value conflicts can also be seen in people's attitudes toward acceptance of environmental risk, and to some degree in hazardous waste facility siting. Milbrath, for example, argues that adherents to the dominant social paradigm, with their "exuberant role toward nature in a competitive market system, urge humans to accept risk in order to maximize wealth." Members of the vanguard "have much greater reservations [about accepting risk] and would proceed with more caution" (Milbrath, 1984: 30). On its face, at least, it appears that members of the rearguard possess a much higher level of environmental risk acceptance than do members of the vanguard.

Although this is no doubt a dimension on which these two groups differ, it is not at all clear how deeply the rearguard's acceptance of risk is seeded. It is clear that these two groups differ with respect to how much risk they believe society should bear in order to obtain the benefits of economic growth. It is much less clear whether these groups differ very much with respect to how much risk they themselves are willing to bear. This is an important distinction to make in trying to understand the NIMBY Syndrome as it applies to efforts to site hazardous waste treatment facilities. The implication of the different risk acceptance postures is that members of the rearguard are less likely to exhibit this syndrome than are members of the vanguard. This places the onus of the NIMBY Syndrome clearly on the vanguard.

It is entirely possible that members of the rearguard, who urge people to accept greater risks, are in a position where they can advocate this approach for others and yet avoid accepting greater risks themselves. This possibility is made stronger by the tendency for the rearguard to have access to greater economic resources.

Milbrath notes that members of the rearguard tend to have relatively high incomes and education levels. A significant segment of this group is made up of business leaders. So the possibility looms that the rearguard exhibits beliefs and behavior that might be said to constitute classic "free-rider" characteristics. They ask others to bear risks while they use their resources to avoid the risks and still receive the economic benefits.

As we noted in Chapter 4, there is very little evidence that socio-economic status by itself plays much of a role in the NIMBY Syndrome. For example, income was less closely related to the NIMBY Syndrome than the perception of health risk, gender, and length of residence. This would tend to imply that perhaps the challengers of the dominant social paradigm are not particularly responsible for the NIMBY Syndrome in facility siting. Although we did not ask questions comparable to those used by Milbrath to identify rearguard and vanguard respondents, in the nationwide survey we did ask a series of questions about opinions toward specific environmental problems. We asked whether each respondent thought that the improper disposal of industrial chemical wastes, pollution in rivers, lakes, and streams, drinking water and groundwater contamination, air pollution from dumps and landfills, and acid rain were problems for the nation as a whole.

Assuming that members of the rearguard are the least likely to consider any of these to be major problems, we can investigate whether such people are the least likely to oppose local facility siting. Table 6.1 presents a breakdown of the people who exhibit the NIMBY Syndrome by their responses to these "problem" questions. These results show a very consistent pattern across nearly all of the problem areas. In general, it appears that people who see these problems as constituting "major problems" for the country are likely to be either opposers or NIMBY Syndromers, but are not very likely to favor hazardous waste facility siting. On the other hand, people who see these as only "minor problems" or "no problem at all" are likely to be either in favor of the facility or generally opposed, but not NIMBY Syndromers.

Although these data do not directly address the issue of whether it is the "vanguard" or "rearguard" which is more likely to oppose siting treatment facilities, it certainly carries some relevant implications. It seems fairly clear that whether people perceive that there are a variety of specific major environmental problems helps to distinguish whether they are likely to favor siting facilities or

Table 6.1
The Relationship Between Perceptions of Environmental Problems and Opposition to Local Facility Siting: Nationwide Results

Attitude Toward Siting	Major Problem	Minor Problem	No Problem
Improper disposal of industrial chemical wastes			
Favor or mostly favor	15.6%	33.3%	100.0%
Generally oppose	48.8	47.2	0.0
Oppose only locally	35.6	19.5	0.0
Total %	100.0%	100.0%	100.0%
n	(334)	(36)	(2)
Pollution of rivers, lakes, and streams			
Favor or mostly favor	11.7%	32.5%	100.0%
Generally oppose	50.0	43.7	0.0
Oppose only locally	38.3	18.8	0.0
Total%	100.0%	100.0%	100.0%
n	(290)	(80)	(2)
Chemicals in drinking water and groundwater			
Favor or mostly favor	11.4%	38.0%	50.0%
Generally oppose	48.4	52.1	25.0
Oppose only locally	40.2	9.9	25.0
Total %	100.0%	100.0%	100.0%
n	(289)	(71)	(12)
Air pollution from smoke stacks			
Favor or mostly favor	9.1%	30.6%	50.0%
Generally oppose	46.9	56.8	20.0
Oppose only locally	44.0	12.6	30.0
Total %	100.0%	100.0%	100.0%
n	(241)	(111)	(20)
Air pollution from dumps and landfills			
Favor or mostly favor	1.1%	30.3%	47.7%
Generally oppose	46.2	58.4	25.0
Oppose only locally	52.7	11.3	27.3
Total %	100.0%	100.0%	100.0%
n	(186)	(142)	(44)
Acid rain			
Favor or mostly favor	5.2%	39.6%	57.7%
Generally oppose	48.4	55.2	23.1
Oppose only locally	46.4	5.2	19.2
Total %	100.0%	100.0%	100.0%
n	(250)	(96)	(26)

whether they will exhibit the NIMBY Syndrome. To the extent that perceiving this variety of specific major environmental problems is associated with being part of the vanguard, then we might infer that the vanguard plays a significant role in opposing the siting of treatment facilities.

The Relationship Between Government and Society

Political theorists have long attempted to formulate prescriptions about the proper relationship between government and the individuals who compose society. Two alternative, almost competing, conceptions of this relationship capture the breadth of difference manifest in American society. In one of these, the concept of "individualism" plays a central role. In the other, the value of "communitarianism" is central (de Tocqueville, 1964; Bellah et al., 1985). Individualism emphasizes the rights of individual people to do as they please with little constraint. It finds its most prevalent manifestation through the assertion of individual property rights. Communitarianism emphasizes social utility and finds its basis in assertions of what is good for public health, safety, and social welfare.

In normative prescriptions emphasizing individualism, government is said to be best when it governs the least. Where communitarianism is emphasized, government's role is said to be to protect the public good and to prevent the exercise of individual rights which have the effect of doing violence to public health, safety, or welfare. These central and competing values find their way into many environmental conflicts and ultimately play a role in hazardous waste facility siting issues.

First, the value of individualism as manifest in property rights itself serves as the basis for conflict. For example, in the typical facility siting process, a business may wish to construct a facility on a piece of land that it owns. The business will typically assert its basic right to build the facility by virtue of the implicit property rights it has in owning the land. This right gives way to the realities of government regulation, where an administrative agency invariably must approve the site and license its operation. This provides abundant opportunity for affected residents to assert their individual property rights, which takes form in the claim that the residents' property rights would be compromised if the business is successful in its siting effort. One need not go beyond the claim that siting such a facility would cause massive decreases in residential property values to see this conflict take shape. Indeed, when we queried people who said they opposed facility siting in their community about why they opposed it, as shown in Table 4.12 in Chapter 4, a small number of people (about one percent of each sample) cited this type of reason.

Second, individualism conflicts with communitarianism in that affected residents justify their opposition to facility siting on the basis of a contention that such a site would constitute an imminent health danger to the entire community. Since, according to this value, government's role is to protect human health and welfare, the business cannot be allowed to site the facility wherever it chooses. We can see the potency of this value in justifications for not wanting treatment facilities. Looking back to Table 4.12 in Chapter 4, we can see that some 76 percent of the respondents in the national sample and 63.4 percent of the combined city samples who do not favor siting a facility in their respective communities oppose it for reasons related to public health, safety, and welfare. These people may at the same time assert their own property rights, but the recognition of limitations on some property rights because of concern for human health may well be a reflection of the latent communitarian values in society.

Distributional Equity: Competing Senses of Fundamental Fairness

While many environmental disputes are rooted in disagreements over the roles of technology, nature, and government in society, some disputes are also rooted in conflicting notions of who should bear the burdens for society's benefits, and how much burden these people should have to bear. Indeed, much of the debate over the priority that should be given to environmental protection during the last decade has carried with it at least implicit notions of distributional fairness. For example, one might argue that the failure of the Reagan administration to take a more aggressive stand in reducing air pollution was motivated by the belief that clean air comes at the expense of jobs and employment. In this view, to improve air quality by, for example, reducing sulphur dioxide emissions would endanger thousands of coal-related jobs. Thus, reductions in acid rain could only be achieved at the expense of those people working in high-sulphur coal producing industries.

As the above example suggests, debates over issues of fairness often carry with them elements of other value-based conflicts, and in many ways resemble the disputes over the role of nature in society. The link to the economy and economic well-being could not easily divorce itself from distributional issues. Specific debates over hazardous waste treatment facility siting are subject to the same types of value-based distributional disputes.

Even so, many of the distributional issues in hazardous waste facility siting are only tangentially related to employment and the economy. This is perhaps especially true because of the lack of any sort of social standards or guidelines about how much burden any one individual should have to bear in order to reap the benefit of a job. Even when the burdens are defined as risk-bearing, there is nothing approaching a clear societal standard. This has led Rayner and Cantor to ask "How Fair is Safe Enough?"(1987).

The recent emphasis on economic compensation in siting efforts is testament to the recognition that distributional issues can be paramount. Economic compensation has at its heart the assumption that some intervention is needed to provide a more equitable distribution of benefits than would otherwise be attained. As we argued in Chapter 2, however, the focus of compensation to date has been on trying to improve the distribution of benefits rather than the distribution of burdens. As we saw then, people tend not to be persuaded by the offer of improved benefits. It seems clear that the more salient debate turns on the distribution of burdens rather than benefits.

Distributional value debates are compounded by elements of the conflict over the proper role of government in society, since many people believe implicitly that individualism brings with it a sense that it is a legitimate exercise of individualism to avoid burdens and let others bear them if one can get away with it. Others believe that it is the proper domain of government to require such "free-riders" to bear a just portion of the burdens. Thus, the stage is set for very real disputes over where hazardous waste facilities should be located.

Fragments of the distributional debate can be seen in the results of the public opinion surveys, especially in the answers people provided for why they oppose local facility siting. These results are again found in Table 4.12. Here we can see that some respondents were very concerned about such issues. When people suggest that the reason they oppose local siting is that "it gives us someone else's waste," "there is already enough here," "it is the producer's responsibility," and "there is not enough land here compared to other places," these are clear statements of belief that they would be asked to bear disproportionate burdens compared to someone else. About 6.8 percent of the respondents in the nationwide sample and some 23.6 percent of the people in the combined Massachusetts sample gave this type of response.

Perhaps equally important, however, is the fact that what would make the local siting inequitable differs from place to place. We know that people who live in relatively rural areas tend to demonstrate more environmental concern than people living in urban or industrial areas (Buttel and Flinn, 1977). In an analysis of the individual Massachusetts city samples, this becomes evident with respect to facility siting. Among those people citing fairness as an issue, those who live in small and rural places (Sturbridge and Ware) clearly articulated a sense that they live in these more rural settings in order to get away from the risks of living in a more industrialized area. To them, they were being asked to bear the burdens for industrial development in Boston and other urban areas. On the other hand, people in the more densely populated areas, especially Chelsea and Brockton, offered the opinion that they were already bearing disproportionately high amounts of society's burden, and that someone else ought to bear the burden for a change. There is no social standard to determine who is correct.

THE PSYCHOLOGICAL CONSTRUCTION OF OPPOSITION

Whatever the values are that underlie disagreements on environmental issues, it is clear that ultimately these values influence the cognitive and affective processes through which people view themselves in relation to the environment. Cognitive psychologists have developed a number of theories to explain the way we tend to perceive the environment. In particular, there has been some important work toward developing theories of environmental risk perception (Covello, 1983). Although it would be impossible to elaborate all of these here, we can review at least a couple of such theories that would seem to have the greatest relevance to hazardous waste facility siting. Initially, we will look at a couple of the most germane theories of risk perception in general. Then we will look at the theoretical and empirical dimensions of risk acceptance, or the attitude of willingness to bear some risks but not others. Each of these types of theories provides some insight into the roots of opposition to facility siting and the NIMBY Syndrome, and each provides a unique description of the magnitude of the problem that public policy must overcome if hazardous waste treatment facility siting is to be a part of that policy.

The Expectancy-Value Theory

Perhaps the best-developed psychological theory of risk perception as applied to noxious facilities is the "expectancy-value" or "expectancy-valence" theory. This type of theory is fairly widely found in studies of organizational psychology. Recently it has been applied to situations involving siting nuclear power plant facilities.

In general, the expectancy-value theory suggests that a "person's attitude toward any object is a function of his beliefs about the object and the implicit evaluative responses associated with those beliefs" (Fishbein and Ajzen, 1975: 29). This is a fancy way of saying that people tend to associate certain properties with specific objects. People's overall attitudes toward a specific object are a reflection of their subjective assessments of all of the properties associated with that object. This theory can also be expressed in terms of a general equation:

$$A_o = \sum_{i=1}^{n} E_i \, V_i$$

where

$A_o =$ the attitude of a person to the object o

$E_i =$ the person's subjective probability that this object will have attribute i

$V_i =$ the person's evaluation (like or dislike) of the attribute i

$n =$ the number of attributes the person associates with object o

This theory can be applied to the attitudes toward a nuclear power plant (or by analogy to a hazardous waste treatment facility). In this case, the nuclear power plant is the object. People tend to associate certain properties or attributes with the nuclear power plant, such as those associated with nuclear weapons, higher or lower electric bills, and many other traits. A person's overall attitude toward the facility is the result of attributes he or she associates with that facility, his or her assessments of the probability that the object is characterized by those attributes, and the extent to which the person likes or dislikes each of those attributes. Different people can develop very different attitudes toward the same object because they can associate different attributes to the object, they can attach different likelihood estimates of the attribute occurring, and/or they can vary in the extent to which they like or dislike the attributes.

In a simple example of a nuclear power plant, a person may associate the facility with a single attribute, destruction from a nuclear weapon. This person's attitude toward the nuclear power plant would then be a function of how likely he or she feels it is that the plant will produce that kind of destruction, and how much he or she likes or dislikes the destruction. This would suggest that before Three Mile Island, when public opposition to nuclear facilities was fairly low (Nealy, Melber, and Rankin, 1983), people assessed the likelihood of nuclear weapon-type destruction to be fairly low, so they had relatively positive attitudes toward such facilities. After Three Mile Island, however, people began to see such destruction as being more likely, and hence their attitudes changed. In actuality, people often attach more than one attribute to a single object, and their overall attitudes consist of a summary of all of these.

The expectancy-value theory of risk perception seems to have some high potential for explaining people's opposition to noxious facilities. This theory has fairly clear prescriptions for the hazardous waste treatment facility siting situation. It suggests that people's opposition might stem from either associating very undesirable properties with the facilities, or assessing the likelihood of undesirable properties as high, or both. In terms of prescriptions for empirical analysis, it points us toward understanding what kinds of properties people tend to associate with hazardous waste treatment facilities and what kinds of probabilities they associate with those properties. The existing research on public opinion toward hazardous waste treatment facility siting has not given us much specific information about either of these attitudinal components.

The Risk Perception Conversion Theory: Dimensions of Risk Acceptance

Another area of psychological research has focused on the process whereby people convert risk "facts" into perceptions of those facts (Slovic, Fischhoff, and Lichtenstein, 1980; Tversky and Kahneman, 1974). This area of analysis has been motivated by the frequent observation that people's assessments of risk usually do not conform to experts' assessments of risk. It seems likely that much more goes into many people's perceptions of risk than the information taken into consideration in expert assessments. Consequently, people are often willing to accept or bear risks that experts evaluate as relatively high, and are often unwilling to accept risks which experts say are relatively low. Why, for example, would many people be willing to accept the dangers of smoking cigarettes, a relatively high-risk activity notwithstanding the addictive qualities of cigarettes, but nonetheless not be willing to buy apples sprayed with Alar (a chemical), which carries relatively low risks? This type of question underlies risk conversion theory.

By investigating the discrepancies between these two forms of risk assessment with respect to activities and events where the risks are fairly well established, researchers have been able to identify a number of factors, sometimes referred to as heuristics, which are related to these discrepancies. In general, there are at least nine different dimensions of risk acceptance, or risk perception factors which affect people's willingness to accept risk. Each of these factors is listed in Table 6.2, along with its more acceptable and less acceptable characteristics. These factors include: how voluntary is the risky action or event; how potentially severe is the action or event; is the event natural or man-made; is the effect immediate or delayed; is the exposure to the risk continuous or sporadic; is the event controllable; is the event relatively new or have people been living with the risk for some time; are the benefits from the risk clear or unclear; and is

Table 6.2
Nine Dimensions of Risk Acceptance

Dimension of Risk Acceptance	If a particular risk is perceived as having these characteristics it will tend to be perceived of as more acceptable	If a particular risk is perceived as having these characteristics it will tend to be perceived of as less acceptable
1. Volition	Voluntary	Involuntary
2. Severity	Ordinary or incremental	Catastrophic
3. Origin	Natural	Human-made
4. Effect-manifestation	Delayed effect	Immediate effect
5. Exposure pattern	Occasional or sporadic exposure	Continuous exposure
6. Controllability	Uncontrollable	Controllable
7. Familiarity	Old, familiar	New, unfamiliar
8. Personal benefit	Clear benefit	Unclear benefit
9. Necessity	Necessary	Luxury

the event a necessity or luxury of life (Litai, Lanning, and Rasmussen, 1983; Rowe, 1977)?

Recent analysis of these nine dimensions suggests that it is often difficult or impossible to attribute risk acceptance to a single perceptual characteristic. For example, when a person's risk-related behavior has more than one risk trait, it is difficult to know whether that person's acceptance of the behavior is due to one or another of these traits (Slovic, 1990). For example, when a person decides to cross a busy street, it is not clear whether he or she is accepting the risks of doing so *because* it is so clearly a voluntary activity, because it is a familiar activity, or perhaps even because there is some clear benefit on the other side. However, as one might expect, empirical estimates of the importance of these nine factors suggest that people are willing to accept or live with events or actions which carry very different levels of risk. For example, a risky action or event which is perceived as being voluntary, uncontrollable, of ordinary severity, of natural or old origin, having delayed consequences, occasional or sporadic exposure, clear benefits, and of some necessity, are less likely to be perceived as risky than actions or events having opposite characteristics.

In a sense, this line of inquiry investigates, at least in part, what influences the subjective probability estimate found in the expectancy-value theory. Thus, the subjective probabilities that specific objects (events or actions) will be risky or dangerous are related to these nine factors. This implies that successful facility siting might be made possible by affecting those factors which can be changed.

We can see how difficult the problem of siting a hazardous waste treatment facility can be when viewed through these nine dimensions of risk acceptance. Given the nature of treatment facilities and most of their associated siting processes, it seems quite likely that people will view such a facility as having most of the properties of unacceptable risk. First, the idea of siting the facility in a particular locale is something that is foisted upon residents, and it is therefore likely to be viewed as involuntary. Second, regardless of how incremental the risk posed by any such facility, people are likely to perceive that this facility will bring with it "new" risks in addition to those already present. Third, the risk associated with the facility is man-made rather than naturally occurring. Fourth, the risk is controllable by its very nature. And fifth, since there is little connection between the operation of a treatment facility and any specific necessity of life, people are likely to perceive that there is no need for treatment facilities. Given this combination of characteristics, it is little wonder that most people oppose treatment facility siting. Although these nine dimensions provide us with a useful heuristic, it is quite difficult to empirically sort out the independent roles played by each dimension. For any given risk action or event, there is likely to be considerable overlap in the presence of traits associated with risk unacceptability. Even so, we can see some of these reflected in people's perceptions of the risks associated with hazardous waste treatment facilities. At least one major element of risk perception theory has tried to apply this to help understand how and to what extent people's perceptions of risk change over time.

Changes in Risk Perception Through a Formal Elaboration of Conversion Theory

More recently, risk perception conversion theory has been formalized to try to describe the specific form of changes people experience when exposed to new or different information. This change-theory suggests that at any given time, changes in people's perceptions of risk from a given activity or event are a function of the perceived risks associated with that activity or event at an earlier time and how any new information is interpreted. This theory focuses on the subjective probabilities that people attach to events that affect them personally. As developed by Viscusi and Magat (1987), this theory has been presented as a general formula:

$$P_{At} = a_B P_{Bt} + a_M P_{Mt}$$

where

P_{At} is a person's perceived risk attached to an event after information is received

P_{Bt} is the person's perceived risk before receiving the new information

P_{Mt} is the amount of risk the person infers from the information

a_B is the personal weight attached to the importance of the event before the new information is received

and a_M is the personal weight attached to the importance of the event after the new information is received.

This formula simply suggests that how people perceive a given event or activity in terms of risk at a given time is a function of how they perceived that event or activity at a prior time plus the perception of the riskiness of that event or activity as inferred from information obtained between the two time points. Thus, how you perceive a nuclear power plant today in terms of risk is a function of how you perceived of it yesterday modified by any risk-related perception that you obtained from new information between yesterday and today.

In general, we have very little directly relevant empirical information about changes in risk perception as it applies to hazardous waste treatment facility siting. Those few studies examining changes in risk perceptions using a more formal change theory have not focused on siting issues, but rather have looked at issues such as radon exposure (Smith, Desvousges, Johnson, and Fisher, 1990; Smith and Johnson, 1988). We can, however, see some possible reflections of this and other psychological theories in the survey results.

A Look at the Psychological Basis of Citizen's Perceptions of Risk From Hazardous Waste Treatment Facilities: Results From the Citizen Surveys

In the best of all worlds, we might like to be able to generate data to test directly the psychological theories and the contextual theories in hazardous waste treatment facility siting. But testing most of these theories would require data that are extraordinarily difficult to obtain. Rather than testing these theories per se, however, we will attempt to make a judgment about whether they seem to hold much potential for improving the siting process by examining the perceptual roots of opposition.

In conducting the analysis of the financial incentives presented in Chapter 2, we also collected information on some aspects of the psychological theories of risk perception. Focusing on the role of risk perception as a psychological trait, we can begin to build a picture of how applicable this type of theory is to hazardous waste treatment facility siting. Again, we really cannot test this theory, per se. Rather, we simply wish to examine the *prima facie* evidence about the role of risk perception from our citizen surveys.

In order to test the expectancy-value theory of risk perception, for example, we would need to ask each respondent questions about the attributes he/she associates with the hazardous waste treatment facility, whether he/she likes these attributes, and assessments of the probabilities that these attributes exist or will occur. We did not do this. Instead, we simply included two risk-mitigating proposals in addition to the financial incentives we discussed in Chapter 2. We selected two risk-mitigating proposals, regular safety inspections and efforts to prevent groundwater contamination. By doing this we can see whether these risk-based proposals seem to hold greater potential for alleviating opposition. If they do seem to hold such potential, we can begin to infer that risk perception plays a fairly significant role in opposition. Perhaps more importantly, we can begin to address the question of what induces people to change their minds about opposing facility siting. The results to these risk-based questions are found in the lower portion of Table 2.4.

Another way of investigating the psychological foundations of opposition involves examining the answers respondents gave to the open-ended question concerning why they oppose siting a treatment facility in their communities. As we will see, the answers that were volunteered have specific contents that allow us to make some inferences about the robustness of the various theories. As we noted earlier, it would not be appropriate to think of this examination as a test of the theories. Rather, we simply wish to investigate the extent to which the various theories seem on their face to offer plausible explanations for, and therefore begin to help us understand, opposition.

We saw in Chapter 2 that, except in Brockton, the risk mitigation proposals (safety inspection and prevention of groundwater contamination) seem to exert more influence on people's benefit/risk assessments than any of the economic incentives. As shown in Table 2.4, even in Brockton, the safety inspection proposal seems to have been the most influential among the proposals, although three of the economic incentives produced slightly greater change than the prevention of groundwater contamination proposal. The result for the nationwide sample is nearly the same. The pattern seems striking. Clearly, the risk mitigating proposals consistently produce greater changes of public sentiment than almost any economic incentive.

We can investigate this even further by re-visiting the range of reasons people gave for opposing local siting of the facility, as shown in Table 4.12. If there is any support for the expectancy-value theory, we would expect to find that people who oppose local siting do so because of some sort of undesirable mental image and high probability of occurrence of that image they associate with the facility.

When we examine the specific answers volunteered by respondents, it becomes fairly clear that many people articulate a vision of severe health consequences. People who refer to reasons for opposition such as "it would contaminate the drinking water," "it would endanger the food," "there is too high a risk of accident," and "it will pollute" really seem to be revealing glimpses of specific pictures they associate with the prospective facility. And because these reasons are so paramount to these people, it seems obvious that they perceive a fairly high probability to be associated with those pictures. Indeed, in some instances, the language that people use to describe these anticipated consequences makes it seem as though they consider the probabilities of occurrence to be 100 percent. Perhaps as many as 15 percent of the respondents explicitly made reference to such specific dire consequences, and had we probed deeper with the respondents who cited high levels of risk and danger, we might well have discovered a much larger set of visual images.

The reasons people volunteered also lend some support to the idea that some of the nine dimensions of risk acceptance are at work here. When people suggest that the reason they oppose local siting is that "we don't need it," one might infer that they perceive the facility to be unnecessary. When people suggest that "local officials can't control safety," and that they "don't trust companies to make it safe," one might read this to mean that the risks associated with the facility are controllable but that in this instance they would not be adequately controlled in practice. And when people respond that they "already have enough" risks to deal with, they may actually be saying that they perceive a facility to carry with it new risks, not only in magnitude but perhaps also in quality.

Again, as was the case with the other psychological theories, there is little information from our surveys that is directly relevant to risk perception change theory. We can nonetheless see how the results we obtained in the survey could certainly be interpreted as being consistent with such theory. For example, when we examined the eleven compensation and risk mitigation proposals, we did so with the expectation that presenting people with new information, information that promised to either compensate them or protect them, might change their minds about opposing facility siting. We expected this new information to be incrementally incorporated into respondents' initially articulated attitudes and perceptions, and our intent was to try to measure the extent to which each proposal affected respondents' perceptions. What we observed, of course, was that the compensation proposals changed very little; the only consistent changes occurred in response to the risk mitigation proposals. Indeed, this is very much what we would expect from the risk perception change theory in that the theory might suggest that new information would only be effective if directed toward perceptions of risks. Only the risk mitigation proposals, by definition, are directed toward people's perceptions of the risks associated with the treatment facility.

Interpreting the Survey Data

To the extent that the psychological theories predict that risk considerations will play a greater role than non-risk considerations in people's attitudes as well as changes in those attitudes, there seems to be some support for these theories. When efforts are promised to reduce risks, there is a somewhat greater tendency for people to express a willingness to change their minds about opposing the facility. This effect may seem even stronger when we consider the possibility that one of the higher-ranking financial incentive proposals, paying for improvements in the quality of fire protection, also carries with it some degree of risking mitigation.

By looking at the reasons people give for their opposition, it seems highly plausible that much of their opposition is fueled by the perception that the proposed facility would carry many of the characteristics of unacceptable risk. It also seems plausible that their perceptions of these characteristics are reinforced by visual images of events or activities that they consider to be highly dangerous and very likely to occur.

We cannot be sure from the data exactly what attributes or probabilities people attach to the treatment facility siting prospect. We have not gone deeply enough into the cognitive content of people's opposition to know whether and to what extent one or another risk perception process is at work. Nor have we been able to determine whether it is because of the risk perception focus of the risk mitigation proposals that these proposals seem to elicit more favorable responses than the compensation proposals. It does seem clear, however, that whatever cognitive processes are at work, the vast majority of people oppose facility siting because of fears of consequent events they associate with negative health effects. It also seems quite plausible that changing people's perceptions of the health risks associated with facility siting may be quite difficult to achieve. Among other things, changes may require that people receive what they perceive to be unambiguously clear information showing that the risks are indeed quite low. Providing this type of information may not be easy or even possible. We need to know much more than we presently do about how people receive information about the risks related to hazardous waste treatment facility siting before we can even make reasonable estimates about the effectiveness of such information.

THE SOCIAL, CULTURAL, AND PSYCHOLOGICAL CONSTRUCTION: A SUMMARY

We have made an effort to review some of the prevalent value bases of disputes over environmental issues. These value bases were extended to situations involving attempts to site hazardous waste treatment facilities. We demonstrated how the disputes are often fueled by disagreements about the role of science and technology in society, the role of nature in society, and the proper role of government in society. These disagreements were also tied to differing views about distributional effects of treatment facility siting, especially who is to bear how much burden or risk. And we made an effort to delve into several prominent risk perception theories to understand the range of views people have about the risks associated with treatment facilities. All of this, combined with the empirical results from Chapter 4, builds a picture of how constrained the siting process is.

It should be clear as a result of the evidence provided here that no single cultural or psychological construction of opposition dominates the decision process. Indeed, opposition to facility siting is very likely fueled by all of the cultural and psychological constraints acting at the same time. The end result, however, is that the majority of people in a given community seem very likely to be opposed to facility siting, albeit for different reasons. Some people oppose such a facility because of fundamental values. Others do so because of their particular psychological construction of risk. Still others probably do so for both reasons. In any event, the reasons why people oppose hazardous waste treatment facility siting appear to be very deeply rooted in contemporary American culture. Moreover, there is very little evidence that any sort of intervention on behalf of the siting process could be capable of changing people's perceptions. If this is so, it is clear that if treatment facility siting is to be a viable part of hazardous waste management and policy, ways must be found to confront these deep-seeded constraints. It is to this that we turn our attention in Chapter 7.

Chapter 7

Solutions to Treatment Facility Siting in an Era of the NIMBY Syndrome: Risk Substitution as a Viable Alternative

Up until now, we have argued that facility siting has not worked, that it has not worked largely because of the emergence of the NIMBY Syndrome, that efforts directed at changing people's attitudes which underlie the NIMBY Syndrome have not worked and are not likely to work in the future, and that the inability to site facilities is fundamentally tied to contemporary American political and social culture, especially the ways in which it leads us to define what are acceptable or fair risks.

What does all of this mean for the future of relying on hazardous waste treatment as part of a comprehensive strategy for hazardous waste management? Does this mean that the issue of siting facilities is essentially intractable? Does it call into question in a fundamental way the wisdom of hazardous waste treatment? Does it suggest that public policy toward the manufacture and disposal of hazardous wastes must be re-thought in its entirety? One might be tempted to draw these conclusions. Yet this is not the conclusion one should take from the argument presented here. Rather, our argument points us to a more incremental alternative or solution—what we will refer to as a risk substitution alternative.

The risk substitution alternative simply prescribes ways that we can respond to the existing political and social contexts in which environmental policy must be formulated, enacted, and implemented. It suggests that we try to understand the nature of existing risks and how people perceive them, and to consider treatment facility siting in this context. Simply stated, risk substitution alternatives point us in the direction of looking for ways that treatment facilities can be sited without significantly worsening individuals' *perceptions* of the risks they face in their everyday lives—and perhaps looking for ways to work toward actually diminishing peoples' real and perceived risks. This is the challenge of risk substitution.

THE OUTLINE OF ALTERNATIVES

Risk substitution alternatives can really only be described in general outline. The nature of the specific substitution of risks is, and must be, completely site and situation-specific. But an outline provides enough general guidance that specific applications naturally flow from it.

Risk substitution suggests that siting hazardous waste treatment facilities starts with an effort to place these facilities into the broader risk context of specific locations. The focus of substitution is on acknowledging that siting the hypothetical facility (at least as practiced to date) can and often does, indeed, represent new, often unfamiliar and unpredictable, risks to people who live in nearby communities. In risk substitution, the emphasis is on finding sites in communities where people are already living with what they consider (or perceive) to be very high, perhaps even unacceptably high, risks. The foundation of risk substitution strategies is the idea that people may well be willing to trade uncertainty about new risks if these new risks are substituted for risks they know or believe to be very high.

In general, the risk substitution strategy calls for parties proposing siting of facilities to analyze specific potential sources of high risk perception, such as existing facilities thought to constitute significant dangers, or recurring or continuous events such as chemical spills or industrial stack emissions, or other environmental problems such as floods or heavy commercial traffic. The idea is to investigate a variety of different kinds and severities of existing activities that might be perceived as being dangerous to local residents and public officials. If a treatment facility siting effort can be oriented toward substituting the potential new risk for some pre-existing specific and identifiable source of the perception of exceedingly high risk in such a community, facility siting becomes much more likely. Table 7.1 contrasts the risk substitution strategies with current practice. In the most promising form of risk substitution, termed "maximal risk substitution," the newly proposed risk would actually work to help diminish existing risks. In other forms, called "minimal risk substitution," the newly proposed risk would add no danger to existing risks.

Maximal risk substitution differs from minimal risk substitution in one major way. Maximal risk substitution possesses a characteristic which might be termed "linkage," in that the risk being substituted is linked in some direct way to the existing risk as perceived by local residents. For example, a hazardous waste incinerator might be located at the site of a Superfund hazardous waste site with the expressed purpose of cleaning up the site. Or a chemical treatment facility might be located at the site of a troubled chemical manufacturing plant. It is with this form of risk substitution that the problems associated with economic compensation, where people perceive that they are being "bought off," are the least likely to occur. With minimal risk substitution, the linkage is less clear, and thus the prospect of engendering the perception of bribery becomes more likely to act as an obstacle to successful siting. We can begin to see how risk substitution might work if we examine a couple of simple examples.

Two Hypothetical Examples

In our first example, we focus on a community which has within its borders one of the many Superfund priority sites around the country. In this particular site, local residents are understandably concerned about the presence of substantial amounts of chemical solvents and other contaminants buried many years ago

Table 7.1
Forms of Risk Substitution Compared to Current Practice

Siting Strategy	Functional Strategy	Risk Perception Implications
Current Practice	New facility is simply added on to the risks faced by nearby residents in the host community.	New facility is perceived as creating an incrementally or substantially increased level of risk over what previously exists. Most residents oppose any new facility.
Minimal Risk Substitution	New facility is substituted for some existing facility or problem where the new facility is perceived as having about equal risks as the existing facility or problem.	New facility is perceived as creating no new or increased levels of risk, although it is perceived as no better than the existing level of risk; most residents are either indifferent to which of the facilities they prefer to live near; some residents prefer the status quo believing "better the risks we know than the ones we don't."
Maximal Risk Substitution	New facility is substituted for some existing facility or problem where the new facility is perceived as having less risk than previously existed.	New facility is perceived as decrementally or substantially lower in level of risk than previously existed; most residents prefer the new facility over the existing facility or problem; some residents still oppose under the belief that the existing risks can be reduced without accepting any new risks.

at the location of a now defunct manufacturing plant. These contaminants have started to show up in the town's groundwater supply, and the town has started to close wells where testing has verified the contamination. The citizens of this community are even more concerned about the lack of governmental action to clean up the wastes. State and federal agencies have been studying the problem for some time, and have determined that remedial action, while justifiable in terms of health risks, is simply too expensive to embark on in the near future.

A party using a risk alternative strategy to siting hazardous waste treatment facilities might find this type of community to be quite willing to accommodate the treatment facility if the first order of business were to clean up the existing site. In this case, the people of the community may be currently living with a risk that they perceive to be too high. They may wish to permit such a facility as a specific means of reducing the risks they perceive they face from the existing Superfund site.

Does this mean that residents living near all existing Superfund sites would be willing to accept a treatment facility? Of course not. For one thing, not all Superfund sites (or hazardous waste sites of any sort) contain wastes which can be treated or are accessible to any kind of existing treatment technology. For another thing, many people simply will not accept the idea that they should have to confront a new set of risks in order to diminish the old. Such people may rather keep fighting for remedial action on the existing site. But we can at least speculate that among all of the communities with hazardous waste sites which are suscep-tible to clean-up with existing technology, there may well be some which are willing that accept this trade-off. The challenge of the risk substitution strategy is to find such communities.

Another example illustrates how this kind of strategy might be employed for other types of existing risks. Let us imagine that the setting for this second example is a middle-sized, mixed-use, but largely residential community. By mixed-use we simply mean that, like hundreds of such communities around the country, the community is not dedicated solely to residential use. Instead, there are a fair number of businesses and a few small light industries. In this community, many people have lived for the last 30 years in close proximity to a chemical manufacturing plant. Until a couple of years ago, few people knew or cared very much about what actually occurred in this plant. That is, until about two years ago when there was a memorable explosion and ensuing fire that caused the local fire department to evacuate an area several miles surrounding the plant. It seems that the chemicals being manufactured in this plant were quite dangerous, and the fumes being given off by the fire were potentially lethal to anyone who might have been downwind.

Since the time of the fire, local officials and residents have come to recognize that the plant poses significant risks for the community. After spending time and money to try to get the plant closed down through legal and political action, and to make the operating environment of the plant difficult by seeking close regulatory agency scrutiny, the plant still operates. This is the type of community which might (and we emphasize the term *might*) be a candidate for risk substitution alternatives.

A party wishing to site a treatment facility in this community using a risk substitution strategy might look for ways that the siting can be done in order to diminish existing risks to local residents. This could possibly be done by purchasing the chemical plant, shutting down its functions, and substituting the hazardous waste treatment functions. Even if not accomplished at the same physical location, as long as people perceive that diminishing the existing risk from the chemical plant can be accomplished by siting the treatment facility, the new facility may become somewhat more palatable.

Does this mean that every community that currently lives with what its residents perceive as extremely high risks would necessarily accept a new facility to replace some older facility? Of course not. Many people would probably continue to believe that the existing facility should be shut down period, and would be unwilling to trade any level of new risk to be rid of the existing risk. Again, the challenge for risk substitution siting methodologies is to identify those communities in which people would be willing to make this trade.

IMPLICATIONS FOR SITING PROCESSES

Perhaps the most important element of risk substitution methodologies is the process used to understand and react to existing risks. It is critical to remember that when we use the term "risks" in the context of this chapter, we are referring to risk perception—which may or may not be related to some definition of actual risks. The key is to remember that what matters is how residents and officials of a given community perceive any proposed facility, and how they perceive the potential trade-off with existing risks or facilities. It would be impossible to suggest that any one type of existing facility would always be traded off by communities for waste treatment facilities. Whether such a facility would be acceptably traded by people in a given city or town is most directly a function of how they perceive the relative risks to themselves and others of concern to them. So the process of implementing a risk substitution strategy starts off by recognizing that although some communities may be more likely to make such a trade-off by virtue of the nature of existing risks, only some communities facing a given type of risk would be expected to be willing to accept a substitute. So the strategy necessarily includes an effort to examine whether there is a willingness to actually trade off existing risks for new risks.

While this idea may not seem fundamentally different from existing practice, it is quite different especially from the perspective of the private sector party wishing to site a facility. We can see this by describing the "typical" siting process and by contrasting what would be necessary under a risk substitution alternative.

In the typical siting process, the effort begins when a private sector party contemplates the construction of a treatment facility. Commonly, a private company from a waste disposal industry will decide that it wants to build a waste treatment facility in a particular state or region. This decision usually results from some internal decision process in which the potential market for the service is established.

Once the decision is made to build a facility, efforts are commonly made to decide exactly where the facility should be built. Usually this decision is made after some type of financial feasibility analysis taking into consideration a variety of factors not unlike those which would be considered by any business contemplating a facility expansion or re-location. These considerations include the cost of, and access to, routes of transportation (such as highways, railroads); the cost of available land; earnings potential due to proximity to local markets; the cost of facility construction; the suitability of given sites in terms of potential environmental impact (making sure, for example, that such a facility is not going to be built on top of a heavily used drinking water aquifer); and the cost of complying with state or local regulations, including environmental regulations such as bans on hazardous materials transport, and non-environmental regulations such as building codes. It is not uncommon, however, for the decision of whether to build to be linked to the issue of where to build, since the where-issue is closely related to cost considerations. When all of the factors are considered, the company may decide to propose building a facility in a given spot which optimizes earning potential at a minimal cost. Rarely, if ever, do cost estimates include the potential time delays which might be encountered from public opposition.

With a risk substitution strategy, consideration of sites must be included early in the process. Instead of conducting financial and feasibility analysis of specific sites in a political and social vacuum, the siting party must conduct some initial analysis of the nature of risk perceptions in communities associated with a number of alternative sites. Such an analysis would begin by trying to determine the extent to which the population in communities containing prospective sites might be averse to a proposed facility. But this analysis must go beyond simply trying to determine which location's citizens seem to be the least opposed.

This initial site analysis must also include a systematic evaluation of existing facilities which *might* pose risks perceived by residents to be very high. Subsequently, it would also include conducting systematic survey research in the communities to ascertain how people perceive the existing facilities and whether there is any reason to believe that residents would be willing to trade one set of risks for another. Then it would include a similar analysis through discussions with local public officials. It might also include conducting series of focus group interviews with community or citizen group leaders to understand exactly the nature of their risk perceptions and willingness to substitute risks. Based on such analyses from a number of potential site communities, an informed judgment can be made about which community is most, and which is least, likely to be agreeable to a risk trade-off. Then a formal proposal can be tailored to the needs and perceptions of the community judged to have the highest potential for success.

RISK SUBSTITUTION IN A NUTSHELL: STEPS IN THE PROCESS

Although each siting effort requires its own form of risk substitution, we can begin to describe the basic steps in the overall strategy that could be pursued by a siting party. These steps begin at the time when decisions are being made about whether, and where, to site particular treatment facilities. It should be made clear from the outset that whatever factors and processes the siting party desires to include must be incorporated into these steps.

Step 1. At the time when alternative sites are being identified (whether for a feasibility analysis, financial analysis, environmental impact assessment, or other purpose), existing facilities, problems, or events which *might* be perceived by local residents as unacceptably dangerous should be identified. At a minimum, an effort should be made to include among the alternate sites at least some which seem to have dangerous facilities, problems, or events which could be redressed as part of a siting proposal. Then, the particular kind of redress should be incorporated into the feasibility and financial analyses of the sites as would probably be done even without a risk substitution strategy.

Step 2. Once the number of sites has been narrowed down to those which are financially feasible, the next step is to make a systematic effort to determine whether local residents and public officials actually do perceive the identified facilities, problems, or events to be unacceptably risky. This can be accomplished through use of a number of social science research techniques, including survey research, focus group interviews, and so on.

Step 3. Once it is established that the existing facilities, problems, or events are indeed perceived as having extremely high risks, the analysis must determine whether these residents and officials would be willing to accept new risks in exchange for eliminating or reducing existing risks. This analysis should not be limited to examining whether people would be willing to trade off some existing risky facility for the proposed treatment facility, but should include analysis of other types of trade-offs people might be willing to make. In this way, the full range of risk perceptions in the respective community can be delineated. Would people be willing to accept a new hazardous waste treatment facility in place of, and in the same location as, an existing chemical plant that had a fire two years earlier? Would residents be willing to allow the treatment facility to be built if the chemical plant were closed? Would residents be willing to accept a new shopping mall in place of some existing risky facility? What about a new police or fire station? How about a new library? In actuality, this kind of analysis can be conducted at the same time as the analysis of risk perceptions associated with existing facilities, problems, or events.

Step 4. Once a fuller picture is created of local perceptions of risk associated with specific facilities (as well as any other information that would be needed, such as a geological assessment, environmental impact assessment, etc.), a proposal can be formulated which seeks to incorporate these perceptions. Primary in such a proposal is the explicit linkage between the newly proposed facility and reduction or elimination of existing risks. Presumably, if the risk substitution strategy is being seriously followed, the proposed risk substitution would be one which is found to be acceptable according to earlier analysis.

Presenting the risk substitution strategy as a series of steps may create the impression that it is easy to implement. This is certainly not the intent. Anyone who has been involved with attempts to site unpopular facilities knows how complex and unpredictable the process can be. And the risk substitution strategy complicates the process, making it perhaps more complex than it was before. The difference, however, is that when risk substitution strategies are employed, there is greater reason to believe that the process will lead to successful siting. Although there is no hard and systematic evidence to this effect, there is scattered anecdotal evidence.

IS THERE EVIDENCE THAT RISK SUBSTITUTION WOULD WORK?

Since risk substitution strategies have not been employed in any systematic way for any particular kind of facility siting, there is no strong empirical evidence that it will work, that is, that people in a local community will openly accept the siting of a hazardous waste treatment facility. Yet there is scattered evidence from a few unwittingly successful siting attempts and some innovative uses of treatment technology that provides more than a ray of hope that risk substitution has formed the basis for success, and can in the future provide a workable solution. Some of the "successful siting efforts" in recent years have apparently benefitted from such a strategy. We can take a closer look at how risk substitution seems to have helped moderate public opposition in two examples. One example is in the report by the New York Legislative Study Commission (1987: 33–36), and the other from the state of Illinois.

In the first instance, although the New York study itself did not address the issue of the role of risk substitution, there seems to have been at least one successful siting effort which benefitted from some sort of substitution—an existing facility was taken out of service to allow a hazardous waste facility siting. It is not possible from the available evidence to know whether this, indeed, constitutes an example of true risk substitution. Much more evidence would have to be generated to clearly establish a risk-substitution link. However, it would appear on its face that there is a strong possibility that this mechanism may have been at work. The second example seems to provide stronger evidence.

Mobile Incineration Units in Illinois

Facing the problem of finding sites for waste treatment, Illinois has experimented with the use of mobile incineration units as part of its overall hazardous waste management policy. Mobile incineration units consist of large trucks which can be transported from place to place in order to incinerate or burn at very high temperatures wastes that cannot be safely disposed of in other ways. Incineration is by no means a perfectly safe or satisfactory means for treating such wastes, but it is arguably safer than other existing methods of disposal. Proposals to build fixed-site incinerators have generally called for burning of wastes from a large geographical area—a region within a state, an entire state, or even a multi-state region. According to the New York State Legislative Commission on Toxic Substances and Hazardous Wastes, incinerators are among the most difficult treatment facilities to site (1987:40). Making incineration units mobile creates a new twist to an old theme.

Part of the rationale for using mobile units is that they tend to be more cost-effective than alternative methods of treatment, especially since their use might obviate the need for public involvement in siting decisions. But it also includes the implication that it is more acceptable to spread the burdens or risks of incineration around to make sure that no single group of people bears the entire burden for waste treatment.

Initial use of mobile units was apparently not met with enthusiasm by local communities. However, when the units were used principally to incinerate only wastes from that local community, there has apparently been less opposition. To the extent that this is true, one might suggest that the reason for the diminished opposition is implicit risk substitution. People may understand implicitly that the use of the mobile units, while certainly not risk-free, constitutes an acceptable trade-off for disposing of, and thereby reducing the risks of, locally produced wastes. Are there alternative explanations for why such units engender less opposition than other types of treatment technologies? There probably are. For example, it might be that when the mobile units process locally produced wastes only, they remain in one place for shorter periods of time. The shorter stay might provide less opportunity for local opposition to develop. However, it is impossible to ignore the possibility and plausibility that it is the risk substitution effect which plays a major role in diminishing local opposition. Clearly, more research needs to be done to examine the empirical linkage between risk substitution strategies and successful siting. Until such strategies are employed, empirical verification will be necessarily limited to case study evidence.

THE BROADER POLITICAL AND SOCIAL CONTEXTS

We have suggested previously that the way we define risks in our society, especially how they are defined at the state, local, and neighborhood levels, plays a major role in shaping opposition to facility siting. Before risk substitution can be said to have any promise of affecting attitudes toward hazardous waste treatment facility siting, we need to address the effectiveness of risk substitution within the context of the political and social construction of risk. Indeed, if it cannot be argued that risk substitution strategies are capable of influencing aspects of or working within the context of the social construction of risk in specific situations, then there may be no reason to think that such strategies will provide an effective vehicle for successful siting.

The appeal of risk substitution strategies is that there is no necessity for people to change the fundamental ways they perceive a given set of risks or their values. It works within the framework of people's perceptions and values rather than trying to change them. It does not attempt to change the way people perceive risks themselves; it does not require that people reassess how they evaluate the risks they are asked to face. Rather, risk substitution promises to alter the political construction of risk itself; it focuses on defining situations in which, consistent with the existing social and political construction of risk, people are willing to have facilities sited. It seeks to identify external conditions under which people would be willing to live with certain levels and types of risks. We can be a little clearer about how and why this is the case by connecting the strategy to some of the elements of the social, political, and psychological construction of risk we discussed in Chapter 6.

We argued in Chapter 6 that there may be fundamental psychological and social reasons why people generally tend to oppose siting hazardous waste treatment facilities. Such opposition seems to be deeply rooted in the contemporary American psyche. It also manifests itself in the variety of social and political values which we hold today. Unfortunately, almost all of the previously attempted "solutions" to siting require that something about the psychological or value basis of people's personal risk assessments be changed. Those proposals which attempt to educate people actually attempt to change individual perceptions of risk. Much of the psychological literature, however, offers little hope that strategies requiring changes in risk perceptions are reasonable in the short run. To the extent that opposition is rooted in the multiplicity of values associated with views about the environment and the role of science in society, many siting reforms actually require that people change their values. This may be a laudable goal in the long run, but again there is little evidence that such value changes can occur over relatively short periods of time. Again, the promise of risk substitution is that it does not require such individual value changes. It merely takes advantage of the existing psychological, social, and political construction of risk as it is currently defined. It does this by identifying situations in which people would be willing to accept the new risks imposed by the siting of a treatment facility in exchange for some older, already existing risks.

An equally compelling aspect of a risk substitution strategy is how it relates to the political system. We have argued throughout

this book that to some degree all existing siting strategies implicitly or explicitly require some type of change in the politics of
siting. Some strategies require more people to participate. Other
strategies are predicated on the requirement that people representing some political interests be systematically excluded from
participation. Risk substitution strategies do not require such
changes in political processes. Rather, they merely attempt to use
existing political processes to help identify risks that are considered by people to be more or less desireable.

It is impossible to escape the implication that relying on risk
substitution strategies will cause residents to be less interested in
opposing proposed facilities. If this is true, then mobilization of
political opposition to facility siting should be less likely—indeed,
it should be less necessary.

LIMITATIONS TO THE RISK SUBSTITUTION STRATEGY

As is the case with nearly all strategies, there are considerable
limitations to the application of risk substitution. First, if the
residents in a local community seriously believe that they can
reduce their risks from existing industry to zero, then no variety
of risk substitution will likely be acceptable to them. Risk
substitution will only work where people perceive that the risks
they face are significant, that these risks are the result of specific
identifiable sources, and that these sources will not likely be
diminished through other interventions or actions. As long as
people believe that the government is going to clean up a
hazardous waste site, there is no incentive for them to accept any
level of new risk as a substitute for the old risk. Of course, the
extent to which people actually perceive that the existing risk can
and will eventually be eliminated is variable across people and
may be variable across communities. Therefore, locating such
people and places is an empirical problem.

A second limitation relates to the role played by the local mass
media. It is not clear how risk substitution proposals would "play"

in the local media. It has been suggested that the local media play a pivotal role in creating opposition to new waste sites (Mazur, 1989). The argument, as we reviewed elsewhere, suggests that the quantity, not the content, of news coverage about a waste site raises public concern about the site and pushes that concern toward opposition. Perhaps residents might come to oppose a facility siting effort regardless of whether the local media are positively or negatively disposed toward a proposal involving risk substitution. The issue, then, becomes one of whether proposals involving risk substitution might engender less media coverage than similar proposals without a risk substitution component. Unfortunately, there is no reason to believe that local media would be any less interested in such a proposal. Whether a proposal with a risk substitution component would work depends on there being a flaw in the relationship between the quantity of news coverage and opposition. Risk substitution probably requires something of a modification to this relationship where people's attitudes can be sensitized to the content of media coverage. Thus, if heavy local media coverage turned out to be very positive in tone toward the elimination of the pre-existing hazard, risk substitution strategies could be successful.

Perhaps the greatest limitation to the use of risk substitution strategies, even if they are successful in allowing facilities to be sited, relates to the broader picture. To the extent that one type of facility is traded for another, the implication is that there could not be any net addition to the number of facilities in operation at a given time. This, of course, would not be a problem if the preponderance of risks eliminated were related to activities or events other than facilities. For example, if hazardous waste treatment facilities were systematically located at Superfund sites, the new treatment facility would indeed constitute a net addition to the existing number of facilities. However, many of the opportunities for risk substitution would probably focus on existing facilities.

Additionally, to the extent that new treatment facilities are substituted for existing facilities, risk substitution strategies might simply shift the problem to another industry or sector of the economy. For example, if a treatment facility were constructed in place of a functioning, albeit problematic, chemical manufacturing facility, the net loss of a chemical plant might simply create the need for an additional chemical plant somewhere else.

APPLICABILITY TO OTHER TYPES OF FACILITY SITING

We have suggested previously that the risk substitution strategy has applicability to the siting of other types of facilities besides hazardous waste treatment facilities. Although there is no empirical evidence brought to bear here on this issue, risk substitution strategies can be applied to a variety of situations. However, the single most important characteristic that any siting effort must have is that the main reason for opposition must be closely related to people's perceptions of the risks involved.

We have argued that the principal reason why people oppose hazardous waste treatment facilities is that such facilities are perceived of as creating substantial risk to their health and property. When this perception is combined with a siting process which ensures that these perceived risks will also be perceived of as new and additional risks, the stage is set for widespread public opposition. Risk substitution strategies build on the nature of people's perceptions of the existing risks they face and the new risk from the proposed siting not being perceived of as adding onto existing risks. So discussion of the applicability of risk substitution for other types of facilities must account for both of these factors: whether the reason for opposition is fundamentally based on risk perception and whether there is any way that the siting process can ensure that the new facility will not be perceived of as adding new risks on top of existing risks.

Many types of facilities attempting to be sited in the U.S. are opposed because of the perception that they pose major risks. Nuclear power generating facilities are probably among the most notable of this type of facility. But many other types of facilities also are opposed for this reason. Siting of prisons, for example, is often opposed because of the fear of escapes. Many types of industrial facilities are opposed because of the fear of environmental contamination they bring, especially those which threaten to release emissions into the ambient air or nearby water. While our focus on hazardous waste treatment facilities has been oriented more toward such facilities as chemical recovery facilities, other types of treatment facilities such as incinerators are also potential subjects for risk substitution strategies.

The fact that the risks are perceived to be high would not seem to be sufficient to conclude that risk substitution might work. The second characteristic has to be present as well. Are there existing risks from facilities or problems which are perceived to be higher than those perceived to be associated with the proposed new facility? If the answer is no, then risk substitution is doomed to failure. It is difficult to imagine what kind of existing risk or facility might be perceived by anyone to be more risky than living near a nuclear power plant. Thus, it does not seem very likely that risk substitution strategies have anything to inform the siting of nuclear power plants. However, it is less clear about other types of facilities.

In our nationwide survey, we investigated whether there tended to be some types of facilities that are more or less desirable for people to live near than a hazardous waste treatment facility. We can examine the answers to the series of questions we asked to see what kinds of patterns of preferences seem to characterize people's perceptions. We asked respondents:

Now, I'd like to ask you how you think you would feel about living *within one mile* of a hazardous waste treatment facility compared to other kinds of facilities. If you had to choose between living *within one mile* of a hazardous waste treatment facility and a state prison, which one would you prefer to live near?

If the respondent initially could not decide, we prompted with "What if you had to choose one or the other?" We repeated this question for preference between a hazardous waste treatment facility and five other types of facilities: a plant which manufactures flammable chemicals; an ammunitions factory; an airport; busy railroad tracks; and a nuclear-powered electric generating plant.

Because of the way in which these questions were asked, we must be careful in our interpretations. The results only tell us how people say they feel about the specific trade-offs between living near a hazardous waste treatment facility and each of the other facilities. It is tempting to examine the aggregate results and to try to infer which type of facility is most preferred, which is preferred second, and so on. However, because we did not ask individuals to tell us which of the non-hazardous waste facilities they would prefer to live near, we might be tempted to infer that preferences are transitive when they really are not. For example, we did not ask people whether they would prefer to live near a nuclear power plant or an airport, and so on. Thus, although in the aggregate there are more people who chose the airport versus a hazardous waste facility than the nuclear power plant versus a hazardous waste facility option, it is possible that if we had asked people explicitly about living near a nuclear power plant versus living near an airport, significant numbers of people might have opted to live near the power plant.

With these caveats in mind, we can examine the basic results of these preferences, as presented in Table 7.2 and Figure 7.1. Here we can see that for every option, there are significant numbers of people who suggested that they would prefer to live within a mile of the hazardous waste treatment facility. As the bar graph in Figure 7.1 shows quite clearly, the alternative to living near a hazardous waste treatment facility which seems to be preferred the least is, as one might expect, living near a nuclear power plant. The alternative that is most preferred over living near a hazardous waste treatment facility is living near busy railroad tracks.

Table 7.2
Patterns of Comparative Preference for Living Within One Mile of Various Types of Facilities*

Alternative	Percent who would prefer to live within one mile of alternative	Percent who would prefer to live within one mile of hazardous waste facility
Living near nuclear power plant	3.3%	90.1%
Living near chemical manufacturing plant	52.8%	37.6%
Living near ammunition manufacturing plant	57.7%	35.0%
Living near prison	68.4%	22.2%
Living near airport	80.1%	11.0%
Living near busy railroad tracks	89.4%	5.3%

* Numbers do not sum to 100% across because of people who responded "don't know."

These results would seem to suggest that, in the aggregate, people who already live near nuclear power plants may be the most likely to be receptive to some form of risk substitution. Of course, it does not seem likely that a developer could conceivably replace a nuclear power plant with a hazardous waste treatment facility. However, this may not be the case with some of the other alternatives. For example, a plant which manufactures flammable chemicals, perhaps especially one that has a history of accidents, might present a particularly salient target for new treatment facility siting. Even without having any particular experience with an accident, significant numbers of people would still rather live within a mile of a hazardous waste treatment facility than a chemical manufacturing facility.

Above all else, these results make it clear that there is a fair range of preference for living near different kinds of facilities. Indeed, we would probably expect this range to be even wider if we had examined a wider range of kinds of alternative facilities.

Figure 7.1
Preferences for Living Near Facilities: Hazardous Waste Treatment Sites Versus Alternatives

Whether living near any of these other types of facilities would actually provide the basis for risk substitution in practice remains to be seen. Specific analysis should be able to determine whether people who live in a particular city or town would prefer to live near a hazardous waste treatment facility rather than near some existing facility of whatever type. This, as we argued earlier, is a critical piece of information that must be incorporated into the siting process.

RISK SUBSTITUTION STRATEGIES: A SUMMARY

We have suggested that risk substitution strategies may well provide some mechanism for helping to successfully site hazardous waste treatment facilities that are now impossible or nearly impossible to site. Such strategies may also hold some hope for other types of facilities. Perhaps the most compelling aspect of this type of strategy is that it does not require that anyone change in attitude, opinion, perception, or behavior to make it work. The strategy builds on current knowledge about why people oppose facilities, but does not seek to use that knowledge for the purpose of changing people's perceptions. Indeed, we have suggested that any framework for siting which requires people to change is likely to be unworkable simply because people's perceptions do not change very much. Instead, the proposed strategy works with the existing knowledge, creating a framework for siting processes which can potentially avoid the sometimes rancorous debate and conflict over the siting of specific facilities.

There can be little question that more research needs to be conducted to identify the extent of past experience with risk substitution practices, even if these experiences may have been the result of site-specific situations. Whether risk substitution strategies work or not remains to be proven. They must be tried and systematically evaluated before more definitive conclusions can be drawn. But unlike any other prescription for siting, this strategy neither seeks nor requires changes in people's perceptions. This fact, combined with scattered evidence from a few successful siting efforts may provide some hope for future siting proposals.

References

Aharoni, Yair. 1981. *The No-Risk Society*. Chatham, NJ: Chatham House.

Allen, Frederick W. 1987. "Toward a Holistic Application to Risk: The Challenge for Communicators and Policy Makers," *Science, Technology, and Human Values*. Vol. 12, Nos. 60 and 61, Summer/Fall, pp. 138–143.

Andrews, Richard N.L., and Terrence K. Pierson. 1984. "Hazardous Waste Facility Siting Processes: Experience from Seven States," *Hazardous Waste*, Vol. 1, No. 3, Fall, pp. 377–386.

Andrews, Richard N.L., and Terrence K. Pierson. 1985. "Local Control or State Override: Experiences and Lessons to Date," *Policy Studies Journal*, Vol. 14, No. 1, September, pp. 90–99.

Arcury, Thomas A., Susan J. Scollay, and Timothy P. Johnson. 1987. "Sex Differences in Environmental Concern and Knowledge: The Case of Acid Rain," *Sex Roles*, Vol. 16, Nos. 9/10, pp. 463–472.

Armour, Audrey, ed. 1984. *The Not-in-my-Backyard Syndrome*. Downsview, Ontario: York University.

Bachrach, Kenneth and Alex Zautra. 1985. "Coping with a Community Stressor: The Threat of a Hazardous Waste Facility," *Journal of Health and Social Behavior*, Vol. 26, pp. 127–141.

Bacow, Lawrence and J.F. Milkey. 1982. "Overcoming Local Opposition to Hazardous Waste Facilities: The Massachusetts Approach," *Harvard Environmental Law Review*, Vol. 6, pp. 265–305.

Bacow, Lawrence, and Michael Wheeler. 1984. *Environmental Dispute Resolution*. New York: Plenum Press.

Baldassare, Mark. 1985. "Trust in Local Government," *Social Science Quarterly*, Vol. 66, No. 3, September, pp. 704–712.

162   *References*

Barber, Benjamin. 1984. *Strong Democracy: Participatory Politics for a New Age*. Berkeley, CA: University of California Press.

Bellah, Robert, *et al*. 1985. *Habits of the Heart: Individualism and Commitment in American Society*. Berkeley, CA: University of California Press.

Berger, Peter, and Thomas Luckman. 1967. *The Social Construction of Reality: A Treatise in the Sociology of Knowledge*. New York: Doubleday.

Berman, Steven H. and Abraham Wandersman. 1990. "Fear of Cancer and Knowledge of Cancer: A Review and Proposed Relevance to Hazardous Waste Sites," *Social Science and Medicine*, Vol. 31, pp. 81–90.

Blocker, T. Jean and Douglas Lee Eckberg. 1989. "Environmental Issues as Women's Issues: General Concerns and Local Hazards," *Social Science Quarterly*, Vol. 70, No. 3, pp. 586–593.

Bowman, Ann O'M. 1984. "Intergovernmental and Intersectoral Tensions in Environmental Policy Implementation: The Case of Hazardous Waste," *Policy Studies Review*, Vol. 4, November, pp. 230–244.

Bowman, Ann O'M. 1985. "Hazardous Waste Cleanup and Superfund Implementation in the Southeast," *Policy Studies Journal*, Vol. 14, No. 1, September, pp. 100–110.

Brion, Denis J. 1984. "Private Property and Social Property," in *Not in My Backyard!: Community Reaction to Locally Unwanted Land Use*. Charlottesville, VA: Institute for Environmental Negotiation, University of Virginia, pp. 43–52.

Brody, Charles J. 1984. "Differences by Sex in Support for Nuclear Power," *Social Forces*, Vol. 63, No. 1, September, pp. 209–221.

Buckle, Leonard, and Suzann Thomas Buckle. 1986. "Placing Environmental Mediation in Context: Lessons from 'Failed' Mediations," *Environmental Impact Assessment Review*, Vol. 6.

Burger, Edward J. 1984. *Health Risks: The Challenge of Informing the Public*. Washington, D.C.: The Media Institute.

Buttel, F.H and W.L. Flinn. 1976. "Economic Growth vs. The Environment: Survey Evidence," *Social Science Quarterly*, Vol. 57, No. 2, September, pp. 410–420.

Buttel, F.H. and W.L. Flinn. 1977. "Conceptions of Rural Life and Environmental Concern," *Rural Sociology*, Vol. 42, No. 4, Winter, pp. 544–555.

Buttel, F.H. and W.L. Flinn. 1978a. "The Politics of Environmental Concern: The Impacts of Party Identification and Political Ideology on Environmental Attitudes," *Environment and Behavior*, Vol. 10, pp. 17–36.

Buttel, F.H. and W.L. Flinn. 1978b. "Social Class and Mass Environmental Beliefs: A Reconsideration," *Environment and Behavior*, Vol. 10, September, pp. 433–450.

Carson, Rachel. 1962. *Silent Spring*. Boston: Houghton Mifflin.

Catton, William R. and Riley E. Dunlap. 1978. "Environmental Sociology: A Paradigm," *The American Sociologist*, Vol. 13, pp. 41–49.

Catton, William R. and Riley E. Dunlap. 1980. "A New Ecological Paradigm for Post-Exuberant Sociology," *The American Behavioral Scientist*, Special Issue, Vol. 24, pp. 15–47.

Cohen, Steven. 1984. "Defusing the Toxic Timebomb: Federal Hazardous Waste Programs," in Michael E. Kraft and Norman J. Vig, eds., *Environmental Policy in the 1980's*. Washington, D.C.: Congressional Quarterly Press.

Collins, R., B. Dotson, C. Lambert, and B. Bailey. 1984. "Locally Unwanted Land Use and Community Reaction," in *Not in My Backyard!: Community Reaction to Locally Unwanted Land Use*. Charlottesville, VA: Institute for Environmental Negotiation, University of Virginia, pp. 1–7.

Condron, Margaret M., and Dixie L. Sipher. 1983. *Hazardous Waste Facility Siting: A National Survey*, June 1987. Albany, NY: Legislative Commission on Toxic Substances and Hazardous Waste.

Cotgrove, Stephen F. 1981. "Risk, Value Conflict, and Political Legitimacy," in R. Griffiths. *Dealing with Risk*. New York: Wiley and Sons.

Cotgrove, Stephen F. 1982. *Catastrophe or Cornucopia: The Environment, Politics, and the Future*. New York: Wiley and Sons.

Cotgrove, Stephen F. and A. Duff. 1980. "Environmentalism, Middle Class Radicalism, and Politics," *Sociological Review*, Vol. 28, No. 2, pp. 333–351.

Covello, Vincent T. 1983. "The Perception of Technological Risks: A Literature Review," *Technological Forecasting and Social Change*, Vol. 23, pp. 285–297.

Dabilis, Andrew J. 1989. "Rivals wooing E. Bridgewater with bids for incincerator site," *The Boston Globe*, Thursday, November 16, p. 92.

Davis, Charles. 1986. "Public Involvement in Hazardous Waste Siting Decisions," Paper delivered at the Annual Meeting of the American Political Science Association, Washington, D.C.: August.

Dietz, Thomas M. and Robert W. Rycroft. 1987. *The Risk Professionals*. New York: Russell Sage Foundation.

Dillman, Don. 1978. *Mail and Telephone Surveys: The Total Design Method*. New York: Wiley and Sons.

Douglas, Mary. 1985. *Risk Acceptability According to the Social Sciences.* New York: Russell Sage Foundation.

Douglas, Mary, and Aaron Wildavsky. 1982a. *Risk and Culture: An Essay on the Selection of Technological and Environmental Dangers.* Berkeley, CA: University of California Press.

Douglas, Mary, and Aaron Wildavsky. 1982b. "How Can We Know the Risks We Face? Why Risk Selection is a Social Process," *Risk Analysis,* Vol. 2, No. 2, pp. 49–51.

Downey, Gary L. 1985. "Federalism and Nuclear Waste Disposal: The Struggle Over Shared Decision Making," *Journal of Policy Analysis and Management,* Vol. 5, No. 1, pp. 73–99.

Dryzek, John S. 1987. *Rational Ecology: Environment and Political Economy.* New York: Basil Blackwell.

Duerksen, Christopher. 1983. *Environmental Regulation of Industrial Plant Siting: How to Make It Work Better.* Washington, D.C.: The Conservation Law Foundation.

Dunlap, Riley E. and William R. Catton. 1979. "Environmental Sociology," *Annual Review of Sociology,* Vol. 5, pp. 243–273.

Edelstein, Michael R. 1987. *Inverting the American Dream: The Social and Psychological Dynamics of Residential Toxic Exposure.* Boulder, CO: Westview Press.

Edelstein, Michael R. 1988. *Contaminated Communities: The Social and Psychological Impacts of Residential Toxic Exposure.* Boulder, CO: Westview Press.

Edelstein, Michael R. and Abraham Wandersman. 1987. "Community Dynamics in Coping with Toxic Contaminants," in I. Altman and A. Wandersman, eds., *Neighborhood amd Community Environments.* New York: Plenum.

Elliott, Michael L.P. 1984. "Improving Community Acceptance of Hazardous Waste Facilities Through Alternative Systems for Mitigating and Managing Risk," *Hazardous Waste.* Vol. 1, No. 3, pp. 397–410.

Elliott, Michael L.P. 1985. "Evaluation of Facility Siting Proposals: The Dynamics of Lay and Analytic Perceptions of Risk in the Siting of Hazardous Waste Management Facilities." Medford, MA: Center for Environmental Management, Tufts University, Hazardous Waste Facility Siting Research Issue Paper.

Fischer, Claude S. 1984. *The Urban Experience.* New York: Harcourt, Brace, and Jovanovich.

Fischhoff, Baruch. 1985. "Managing Risk Perceptions," *Issues in Science and Technology,* Fall, pp. 83–96.

Fischhoff, Baruch, Paul Slovic, and Sarah Lichtenstein. 1983. " 'The Public' Vs. 'The Experts': Perceived Vs. Actual Disagreements

About the Risks of Nuclear Power," in Vincent T. Covello, W. Gary Flamm, Joseph V. Rodricks, and Robert G. Tardiff, eds., *The Analysis of Actual Versus Perceived Risks*. New York: Plenum Press, pp. 235–249.

Fischhoff, Baruch, Paul Slovic, Sarah Lichtenstein, S. Read, and B. Combs. 1978. "How Safe is Safe Enough? A Psychometric Study of Attitudes Towards Technological Risks and Benefits," *Policy Sciences*, Vol. 9, pp. 127–152.

Fishbein, M. and I. Ajzen. 1975. *Belief, Attitude, Intention, and Behavior: An Introduction to Theory and Research*. Reading, MA: Addison-Wesley.

Fortuna, Richard, and David Lennett. 1987. *Hazardous Waste Regulation, the New Era: An Analysis and Guide to RCRA and the 1984 Amendments*. New York: McGraw Hill.

Francis, R.S. 1983. "Attitudes Toward Industrial Pollution, Strategies for Protecting the Environment, and Environmental-Economic Trade-offs," *Journal of Applied Social Psychology*, Vol. 13, pp. 310–327.

Freudenberg, William R. and Rodney K. Baxter. 1984. "Host Community Attitudes Toward Nuclear Power Plants: A Reassessment," *Social Science Quarterly*, Vol. 65, No. 4, December, pp. 1129–1136.

George, David L. and Priscilla L. Southwell. 1986. "Opinion on the Diablo Canyon Nuclear Power Plant," *Social Science Quarterly*, Vol. 67, No. 4, pp. 722–735.

Goetze, David. 1982. "A Decentralized Mechanism for Siting Hazardous Waste Disposal Facilities," *Public Choice*, Vol. 39, pp. 361–370.

Greenberg, Michael R., and Richard F. Anderson. 1984. *Hazardous Waste Sites: The Credibility Gap*. New Brunswick, NJ: Center for Urban Policy Research, Rutgers University.

Hadden, Susan and Jared Hazelton. 1980. "Public Policies Toward Risk," *Policy Studies Journal*, Vol. 9, No. 1, pp. 109–117.

Hadden, Susan, Joan Veillette, and Thomas Brandt. 1983. "State Roles in Siting Hazardous Waste Disposal Facilities: From State Preemption to Local Veto," in James P. Lester and Ann O'M. Bowman, eds, *The Politics of Hazardous Waste Management*. Durham, NC: Duke University Press, pp. 196–211.

Hamilton, Lawrence C. 1985a. "Concern About Toxic Wastes: Three Demographic Predictors," *Sociological Perspectives*, Vol. 28, pp. 463–486.

Hamilton, Lawrence C. 1985b. "Who Cares About Water Pollution? Opinions in a Small-Town Crisis," *Sociological Inquiry*, Vol. 55, pp. 170–181.

Hansen, Susan B. 1984. "On the Making of Unpopular Decisions: A Typology and Some Evidence," *Policy Studies Journal*, Vol. 13, No. 1, pp. 23–43.

Hayes, Pat. 1984. "Comments," in A. Armour, ed., *The Not-in-My-Backyard Syndrome*. Downsview, Ontario: York University Press.

Ingram, Helen, and S.J. Ullery. 1977. "Public Perception in Environmental Decision-making: Substance or Illusion?," in W.R.D. Sewell and J.T. Coppock, eds., *Public Participation in Planning*. New York: John Wiley, pp. 123–139.

Institute for Environmental Negotiation. 1984. *Not in My Backyard!: Community Reaction to Locally Unwanted Land Use*. Charlottesville, VA: Institute for Environmental Negotiation, University of Virginia.

Kasperson, Roger E. 1986a. "Six Propositions on Public Participation and Their Relevance for Risk Communication," *Risk Analysis*, Vol. 6, No. 3, pp. 275–281.

Kasperson, Roger E. 1986b. "Hazardous Waste Facility Siting: Community, Firm, and Government Perspectives," in National Academy of Engineering, *Hazards: Technology and Fairness*. Washington, D.C.: National Academy Press.

Kraft, Michael and Ruth Kraut. 1985. "The Impact of Citizen Participation on Hazardous Waste Policy Implementation: The Case of Clermont County, Ohio," *Policy Studies Journal*, Vol. 14, No. 1, September, pp. 52–61.

Kraft, Michael and Norman Vig, eds. 1988. *Technology and Politics*. Durham, NC: Duke University Press.

Krimsky, Sheldon, and Alonzo Plough. 1988. *Environmental Hazards: Communicating Risks as a Social Process*. Dover, MA: Auburn House.

Kunreuther, Howard, Paul Kleindorfer, Peter Knez, and Rudy Yaksick. 1987. "A Compensation Mechanism for Siting Noxious Facilities: Theory and Experimental Design," *Journal of Environmental Economics and Management*, Vol. 14, pp. 371–383.

Lake, Robert W. 1987. *Resolving Locational Conflicts*. New Brunswick, NJ: Rutgers University Press.

Lave, Lester and Thomas Romer. 1983. "Specifying Risk Goals: Inherent Problems with Democratic Institutions," *Risk Analysis*, Vol. 3, pp. 217–227.

Lester, James P., and Ann O'M. Bowman. 1983. *The Politics of Hazardous Waste Management*. Durham, NC: Duke University Press.

Levine, Adeline Gordon. 1982. *Love Canal: Science, Politics, and People*. Lexington, MA: Lexington Books.

Lipset, Seymour Martin, and William Schneider. 1983. *The Confidence Gap*. New York: The Free Press.

Litai, D., D.D. Lanning, and N.C. Rasmussen. 1983. "The Public Perception of Risk," in Vincent T. Covello, W. Gary Flamm, Joseph V. Rodricks, and Robert G. Tardiff, eds., *The Analysis of Actual Versus Perceived Risks*. New York: Plenum Press, pp. 213–224.

MacDonald, H. Ian. 1984. "Welcome Address," in A. Armour, ed., *The Not-in-My-Backyard Syndrome*. Downsview, Ontario: York University Press.

McStay, J.R. and R.E. Dunlap. 1983. "Male-Female Differences in Concern for Environmental Quality," *International Journal of Women's Studies*, Vol. 6, No. 4, pp. 291–301.

Mansbridge, Jane J. 1980. *Beyond Adversary Democracy*. New York: Basic Books.

Massachusetts Department of Environmental Management. 1982. Bureau of Solid Waste Disposal. *Hazardous Waste Management in Massachusetts: 1982 Statewide Environmental Impact Report*. Boston, MA: Massachusetts Department of Environmental Management.

Matheny, Albert R. and Bruce A. Williams. 1985. "Knowledge Vs. NIMBY: Assessing Florida's Strategy for Siting Hazardous Waste Disposal Facilities," *Policy Studies Journal*, Vol. 14, No. 1, September, pp. 70–80.

Mazmanian, Daniel A., and David Morell. 1988. "The Elusive Pursuit of Toxics Management," *The Public Interest*, No. 90, Winter, pp. 81–98.

Mazmanian, Daniel A., Michael Stanley-Jones, and Miriam J. Green. 1988. *Breaking Political Gridlock: California's Experiment in Public-Private Cooperation for Hazardous Waste Policy*. Claremont, CA: California Institute of Public Affairs.

Mazur, Allan. 1981. *The Dynamics of Technical Controversy*. Washington, D.C.: Communications Press.

Mazur, Allan. 1989. "Communicating Risk in the Mass Media," in D. Peck, ed. *Psychological Effects of Hazardous Toxic Waste Disposal on Communities*. Springfield, IL: Charles C. Thomas, pp. 119–137.

Merchant, C. 1980. *The Death of Nature: Women, Ecology, and the Scientific Revolution*. San Francisco, CA: Harper and Row.

Milbrath, Lester. 1984. *Environmentalists: Vanguard for a New Society*. Albany, NY: State University of New York Press.

Mitchell, Robert C. 1984. "Rationality and Irrationality in the Public's Perception of Nuclear Power," in W.R. Freudenberg and E.A. Rosen, eds., *Public Reaction to Nuclear Power: Are There Critical Masses?* Boulder, CO: Westview Press, pp. 137–179.

Mitchell, Robert Cameron, and Richard T. Carson. 1986. "Siting Hazardous Facilities: Property Rights, Protest, and the Siting of Hazardous

Waste Facilities," *American Economics Association Papers and Proceedings*, Vol. 76, No. 2, May, pp. 285:290.

Mohai, Paul. 1985. "Public Concern and Elite Involvement in Environmental-Conservation Issues," *Social Science Quarterly*, Vol. 66, No. 4, December, pp. 820–838.

Morell, David, and Christopher Magorian. 1982. *Siting Hazardous Waste Facilities: Local Opposition and the Myth of Preemption.* Cambridge, MA: Ballinger Press.

Morone, Joseph G., and Edward J. Woodhouse. 1986. *Averting Catastrophe: Strategies for Regulating Risky Technologies.* Berkeley, CA: University of California Press.

National Research Council. 1983. *Risk Assessment in the Federal Government: Managing the Process.* Washington, D.C.: National Academy Press.

Nealy, Stanley M., Barbara D. Melber, and William L. Rankin. 1983. *Public Opinion and Nuclear Energy.* Lexington, MA: Lexington Books.

New York Legislative Commission on Toxic Substances and Hazardous Wastes. 1987. *Hazardous Waste Facility Siting: A National Survey June, 1987.* Albany, NY.

O'Hare, Michael. 1977. " 'Not on My Block You Don't' - Facilities Siting and the Importance of Compensation," *Public Policy*, Vol. 25, pp. 407–459.

O'Hare, Michael. 1984. "Governments and Source Reduction of Hazardous Waste," *Hazardous Waste*, Vol. 1, No. 3, pp. 443–451.

O'Hare, Michael, Lawrence Bacow, and Debra Sanderson. 1983. *Facility Siting.* New York: Van Nostrand.

Ophuls, William. 1977. *Ecology and the Politics of Scarcity.* San Francisco, CA: W.H. Freeman.

Otway, Harry and Kerry Thomas. 1982. "Reflections on Risk Perception and Policy," *Risk Analysis*, Vol. 2, No. 2, pp. 69–82.

Otway, Harry. 1987. "Experts, Risk Communication, and Democracy," *Risk Analysis*, Vol. 7, No. 2, pp. 125–129.

Passino, E.M. and J.W. Lounsbury. 1976. "Sex Differences in Opposition to and Support for Construction of a Proposed Nuclear Power Plant," in P. Suedefelf and J.A. Russell, eds., *The Behavioral Basis of Design*, Book 1, Selected Papers. Dowden, Hutchinson, and Ross.

Peck, D., ed. 1989. *Psychological Effects of Hazardous Toxic Waste Disposal on Communities.* Springfield, IL: Charles C. Thomas.

Perrow, Charles. 1984. *Normal Accidents: Living with High Risk Technologies.* New York: Basic Books.

Plough, Alonzo, and Sheldon Krimsky. 1987. "The Emergence of Risk Communication Studies: Social and Political Context," *Science,*

Technology, and Human Values, Vol. 12, Nos. 3 and 4, Summer/Fall, pp. 4–10.

Popper, Frank J. 1981. "Siting LULU's," *Planning*. Vol. 47, April, pp. 12–15.

Portney, Kent E. 1983. *Citizen Attitudes Toward Hazardous Waste Facility Siting: Public Opinion in Five Massachusetts Communities*. Medford, MA: Lincoln Filene Center for Citizenship and Public Affairs, Tufts University.

Portney, Kent E. 1984. "Allaying the NIMBY Syndrome: The Potential for Compensation in Hazardous Waste Treatment Facility Siting," *Hazardous Waste*, Vol. 1, No. 3, pp. 411–421.

Portney, Kent E. 1985. "The Potential of the Theory of Compensation for Mitigating Public Opposition to Hazardous Waste Treatment Facility Siting: Some Evidence from Five Massachusetts Communities," *Policy Studies Journal*, Vol. 14, No. 1, pp. 81–89.

Portney, Kent E. 1986. "The Perception of Health Risk and Opposition to Hazardous Waste Treatment Facility Siting: Implications for Hazardous Waste Management and Policy from Survey Research," in *Papers and Proceedings of the Applied Geography Conferences*, Vol. 9, pp. 114–123.

Portney, Kent E. 1990. "The Dilemma of Democracy in Local Hazardous Waste Treament Facility Siting," in John Havick, ed., *Mass Communications, Democratization, and the Political Process*. Westport, CT: Greenwood Press.

Rayner, Steve. 1984. "Disagreeing About Risk: The Institutional Cultures of Risk Management and Planning for Future Generations," in Susan Hadden, ed., *Risk Analysis, Institutions, and Public Policy*. New York: Associated Faculty Press.

Rayner, Steve and Robin Cantor. 1987. "How Fair is Safe Enough? The Cultural Approach to Societal Technological Choice," *Risk Analysis*, Vol. 7, No. 1, pp. 3–13.

Rosenbaum, Walter A. 1983. "The Politics of Public Participation in Hazardous Waste Management," in James P. Lester and Ann O'M. Bowman, eds., *The Politics of Hazardous Waste Management*. Durham, NC: Duke University Press, pp. 176–195.

Rowe, William D. 1977. *The Anatomy of Risk*. New York: John Wiley.

Ryan, Ann Sprightley. 1984. *Approaches to Hazardous Waste Facility Siting in the United States*. Report to the Massachusetts Hazardous Waste Facility Site Safety Council. Boston, MA: Massachusetts Hazardous Waste Facility Site Safety Council.

Sagoff, Mark. 1984. "Nine Propositions on NIMBIES or Learning from the Tiv," in Institute for Environmental Negotiation. *Not in My Backyard!: Community Reaction to Locally Unwanted Land Use*. Charlottesville, VA: Institute for Environmental Negotiation, University of Virginia, pp. 55–63.

Sandman, Peter D. 1986. "Getting to Maybe: Some Communications Aspects of Hazardous Waste Facility Siting," *Seton Hall Legislative Journal*, Vol. 9, No. 2, Spring, pp. 437–465.

Schwartz, Steven P., Paul E. White, and Robert G. Hughes. 1985. "Environmental Threats, Communities, and Hysteria," *Journal of Public Health Policy*, Vol. 3, March, pp. 58–77.

Simmons, John. 1984. "Rights and Wrongs in Hazardous Waste Disposal," in *Not in My Backyard!: Community Reaction to Locally Unwanted Land Use*. Charlottesville, VA: Institute for Environmental Negotiation, University of Virginia, pp. 11–19.

Slovic, Paul. 1990. "Perception of Risk: Reflection on the Psychometric Paradigm," Paper Presented at the Workshop on Risk and Risk Communication, Tufts University, January 11–12.

Slovic, Paul, Baruch Fischhoff, and Sarah Lichtenstein. 1980. "Facts and Fears: Understanding Perceived Risk," in R. Schwing and W. Albers, eds., *Societal Risk Assessment: How Safe is Safe Enough?* New York: Plenum Press, pp. 181–216.

Smith, M.A., F.M. Lynn, R.N.L. Andrews, R. Olin, and C. Maurer. 1985. *Costs and Benefits to Local Governments Due to Presence of a Hazardous Waste Management Facility and related Compensation Issues*. Chapel Hill, NC: University of North Carolina Institute for Environmental Studies.

Smith, V. Kerry, William H. Desvousges, F. Reed Johnson, and Ann Fisher. 1990. "Can Public Information Programs Affect Risk Perception?" *Journal of Policy Analysis and Management*, Vol. 9, No. 1, pp. 41–59.

Smith, V. Kerry and F. Reed Johnson. 1988. "How Do Risk Perceptions Respond to Information?" *Review of Economics and Statistics*, Vol. 70, May, pp. 1–8.

Snow, C.P. 1960. *The Two Cultures and the Scientific Revolution*. New York: Cambridge University Press.

Snow, C.P. 1964. *The Two Cultures; and a Second Look*. New York: University Press.

Spain, Daphne. 1984. "Women's Role in Opposing Locally Unwanted Land Uses," in *Not in My Backyard!: Community Reaction to Locally Unwanted Land Use*. Charlottesville, VA: Institute for Environmental Negotiation, University of Virginia, pp. 33–40.

Starr, Chauncey. 1969. "Social Benefit versus Technological Risk," *Science*, No. 165, pp. 1232–1238.

Starr, Chauncey, Richard Rudman, and Chris Whipple. 1976. "Philosophical Basis for Risk Analysis," *Annual Review of Energy*, Vol. 1, pp. 629–662.

Stout-Wiegand, Nancy and Roger B. Trent. 1983. "Sex Differences in Attitudes Toward New Energy Resource Developments," *Rural Sociology*, Vol. 48, pp. 637–646.

Talbot, Allan R. 1983. *Settling Things: Six Case Studies in Environmental Mediation*. Washington, D.C.: The Conservation Foundation.

Thomas, Lee. 1986. "Risk Communication: Why We Must Talk About Risk," *Environment*, Vol. 28, No. 40, March, pp. 4–5.

Thompson, Michael, and Aaron Wildavsky. 1982. "A Proposal to Create a Cultural Theory of Risk," in Kunreuther and Ley, eds., *The Risk Analysis Controversy: An Institutional Perspective*. Berlin: Springer Publishers, pp. 145–161.

Tocqueville, Alexis de. 1964. *Democracy in America*. New York: Washington Square Press.

Tversky, Amos and Daniel Kahneman. 1974. "Judgment under Uncertainty: Heuristics and Biases," *Science*, No. 185, pp. 1124–1131.

USEPA. 1979. *Siting of Hazardous Waste Management Facilities and Public Opinion*. Washington, D.C.: EPA and Centaur Associates, November, Report SW-809.

USNRC. 1975. *Reactor Safety Study: An Assessment of Accident Risks in U.S. Commercial Nuclear Power Plants*. Washington, D.C.: U.S. Nuclear Regulatory Commission, October.

Van Liere, Kent D., and Riley E. Dunlap. 1980. "The Social Bases for Environmental Concern," *Public Opinion Quarterly*, Vol. 44, pp. 181–197.

Viscusi, W. Kip and Wesley A. Magat. 1987. *Learning About Risk*. Cambridge, MA: Harvard University Press.

Vyner, Henry. 1988. *Invisible Trauma: The Psychosocial Effects of the Invisible Environmental Contaminants*. Lexington, MA: Lexington Books.

Wedge, Bryant. 1984. "The NIMBY Complex: Some Psychopolitical Considerations," in *Not in My Backyard!: Community Reaction to Locally Unwanted Land Use*. Charlottesville, VA: Institute for Environmental Negotiation, University of Virginia, pp. 23–30.

Wells, Donald T. 1982. "Site Control of Hazardous Waste Facilities," *Policy Studies Review*, Vol. 1, No. 4, pp. 728–735.

White, Lynn, Jr. 1967. "The Historical Roots of Our Ecological Crisis," *Science*, Vol. 155, pp. 1203–1207.

Wildavsky, Aaron, and Mary Douglas. 1982. *Risk and Culture*. Berkeley, CA: University of California Press.

Williams, Anne S., Patrick C. Jobes, and C. Jack Gilbert. 1986. "Gender Roles, Marital Status, and Urban-Rural Migration," *Sex Roles*, Vol. 15, Nos. 11/12, pp. 627–643.

Wilson, Richard, and E.A.C. Crouch. 1987. "Risk Assessment and Comparisons: An Introduction," *Science*, No. 236, pp. 267–270.

Wynne, Brian. 1982. "Institutional Mythologies and Dual Societies in the Management of Risk," in Kunreuther and Ley, eds., *The Risk Analysis Controversy: An Institutional Perspective*. Berlin: Springer Publishers, pp. 127–143.

Index

U.S. Environmental Protection Agency (EPA), 3, 6, 8, 17, 88, 171
U.S. Nuclear Regulatory Commission (USNRC), 171

value conflicts and siting decisions, 110
value-neutrality in risk assessment, the myth of, 113
vanguard of environmental values, 115–19
Van Liere, Kent D., 76, 171
Veillette, Joan, 8, 50, 165
Vig, Norman, 113, 166
Viscusi, W. Kip, 129, 171
voting on compensation, 55
Vyner, Henry, 171

Wandersman, Abraham, 80, 88, 162, 164
Ware, Mass., 18, 28, 30, 36, 122
waste minimization strategies, 6
Wedge, Bryant, 171
Wells, Donald T., 8, 171

West Germany, environmental values in, 115
Wheeler, Michael, 161
Whipple, Chris, 171
White, Lynn, 115, 171
White, Paul, 170
Wildavsky, Aaron, 110, 164, 171
Williams, Anne S., 80, 172
Williams, Bruce A., 52, 53, 54, 55, 57, 167
Wilson, Richard, 113, 172
Wisconsin, approach to siting, 10
women and the environment, 75. *See also* gender gap
Woodhouse, Edward J., 113, 168
Wynne, Brian, 113, 172

Yaksick Rudy, 36, 55, 166
Yonkers, N.Y., siting low income housing in, 14

Zautra, Alex, 14, 161
zero-sum decisions, siting decisions as, 42, 50, 66

ABOUT THE AUTHOR

KENT E. PORTNEY is Associate Professor of Political Science and Director of the Citizen Survey Program at Tufts University. He is co-author of *The Distributional Impact of Public Policies* and author of *Approaching Public Policy Analysis: An Introduction to Policy and Program Research*. He has also written articles for *Hazardous Waste and Hazardous Materials*, *Policy Studies Journal*, and the *Journal of Voluntary Action Research*.